The Heart Sell

A guide for women entrepreneurs
seeking financial freedom.

By Dora Rankin

© 2024 Dora Rankin

This book is the intellectual property of Dora Rankin and may not be reproduced or distributed without permission. For questions or speaking and media inquiries, email dora@dorarankin.com or visit dorarankin.com.

ISBN: 9798327585249

First Edition

"There is no greater gift you can give or receive than to honor your calling. It's why you were born. And how you become most truly alive."
—Oprah Winfrey

Growth Strategist and Certified Business Coach

DORA *Rankin*
CELEBRATING 25 YEARS OF EMPOWERING WOMEN

I've written this book as a love letter to the memory of my mother, Barbara.

I'd like to shine a spotlight on the millions of women, including my incredible daughters, Anna and Alli, who, like so many, refuse to wave the white flag. They are breaking through barriers to gain equal pay, rights, and power.

We rise together because someday we will rule the world.

Table Of Contents

Introduction

Section One: Follow Your Heart
Chapter 1   What Is "The Heart Sell?" 3
Chapter 2   Why I Love Helping Women Who Are Struggling 15
Chapter 3   My Evil Sidekick 21
Chapter 4   Why Do You Need To Know This About Me? 25
Chapter 5   You Can't Teach Passion 31

Section Two: Championing Women
Chapter 6   The Hard Sell Vs. The Heart Sell 45
Chapter 7   Have You Ever Felt Lost? 55

Section Three: Building Relationships
Chapter 8   Find Your Audience 65
Chapter 9   The Key To Your Heart 75
Chapter 10   Consider a "Sales First" Approach 85

Section Four: You Are The Expert
Chapter 11   Loving Your Business 97
Chapter 12   How To Have A Non-Salesy Sales Conversation 109
Chapter 13   The Art Of Pitch-Free Prospecting (With Heart) 117

Section Five: Client Results
Chapter 14   Switching Gears 127
Chapter 15   Don't Take Failure Personally 135
Chapter 16   Charging What You're Worth 143
Chapter 17   You've Come A Long Way 149

Section Six: The Sky's The Limit
Chapter 18   How To Build A Relationship-Driven, Revenue-Rich Business 159
Chapter 19   Women Who Soar 171

About The Author 177

Introduction

As a business coach for women, I'm on a mission to close the wealth gap for entrepreneurs (like you!) by helping you build a purpose-driven business while becoming financially free.

Did you know that 70% of women business owners make less than $100K per year? Only 2% break the million-dollar mark. I'm on my way to joining that 2%, and I want to take you there with me by helping you create a business built and led from the heart.

The Heart Sell is based on my 25 years of experience empowering women and leading sales teams to build relationship-driven, revenue-rich businesses.

Inspiring Women To Become Self-Sufficient

After 17 years in corporate banking, I decided to pursue a leadership role with a new fintech (financial/technology) startup. We were an unknown company with an unknown product (debt crowdfunding) in a new market.

This was my chance to get more money into the hands of underrepresented women business owners that the banks overlooked. I was determined to make it work, even though I was selling a mysterious new product to people who didn't know the service—or our company—existed.

Today, my mission is born of these same roots. I coach business owners to get more money into the hands of industrious women, especially BIPOC (black, indigenous, and other people of color) women.

I walk my clients—with new businesses or updated products and services—through the process of exploring who their potential clients may be while uncovering new markets. In my world, $100K months are made possible with a combination of strategic sales, lead generation, and smart marketing plans. (If I can teach loan officers sales and lead generation, I can teach you, too!)

I love helping women increase their earnings and grow their businesses so they can make a more significant impact on their world. Together, we create a sales system that generates a steady flow of leads without relying on social media, sales funnels, or paid ads.

Creating Financial Freedom

The Heart Sell helps people grow their businesses by building relationships through sincere conversations that bring them joy. Because this sales method comes from the heart, it gives women business owners a keen advantage.

There is so much noise out there, so many shiny objects, and so much happening online that we overlook the profound power of simply being authentic and connected. After all, there's no substitute for human connection.

Selling Your Products Doesn't Have To Be Hard. Or Gross. Or Scary.

If you want to learn how to walk someone down a path where you can solve a problem for them while invoicing your first $60K or building your million-dollar business—as my clients have—join me. I'll show you how to do it without ads, funnels, or freebies.

I'm so glad you're here. I know you can do this!

XO,
Dora

Growth Strategist and Hello7 Certified Business Coach

P.S. Download free resources to accompany this book at dorarankin.com/book-bundle.

Section One
Follow Your Heart

Dora Rankin

CHAPTER 1
What Is "The Heart Sell?"

If you're a business owner who cringes at the idea of "selling," you're not alone. As a business coach and mentor who guides entrepreneurs to make life-changing amounts of money, I know you'll love the concept behind The Heart Sell. It comes from a place of passion and purpose, built from 25 years of proven methods.

Have you ever found yourself at a networking event, conference, or Zoom chat wondering how to connect with a stranger besides commenting on their lovely attire? If so, The Heart Sell method will grant you access to uncovering an opportunity within any conversation with a step-by-step strategy for relationship selling.

It's a phenomenon that is redefining the world of sales as we know it—especially for women business owners.

Learn How To Make Life-Changing Income

Whether you're considering starting a business or you've been a business owner for years, have you ever considered earning $100,000 in sales in a single month? If you laugh or balk at this question, that tells me you don't think it's possible.

I'm here to tell you it is.

The single most important thing about running a business is sustaining it—and yourself. But there is so much misinformation online about how to start and grow a business, leading entrepreneurs to believe that "if you build it, they will come."

For example, many business coaches will tell you that if you develop an online presence with a website, lead magnet, or online course and combine it with paid advertising to showcase your brand, you've done all the work and can now sit back and watch the dollars roll in.

But that's not the reality, which is why so many women are failing, and that's when they seek my guidance.

So, why isn't it working?

Building a successful business is about more than creating content. It's about something much bigger: building relationships with other human beings. While online programs have their place, they omit the most critical part of the business equation: interacting with the people who need your products and services.

Consider this: Who is better at *building and nurturing relationships* than women? You could say it's one of our unfair advantages. (Sorry, boys!)

Even though a website is a necessary tool in your marketing toolbox, it doesn't guarantee that you will sell a single product. And if you *only* pursue online strategies, you will need a separate budget of thousands—or tens of thousands—to spend on paid advertising.

The problem is that most entrepreneurs can't make that investment and just "hope it will all work out." Hope isn't a strategy—but I've got good news: You don't need to spend thousands on marketing to have robust sales.

From Passion To Purpose To Profit

Why is discovering your life's passion the key to creating a business rooted in purpose? Because it will help you identify fulfilling work that will allow you and your company to thrive. By doing what you love and watching how your products and services help people, you will grow your business and your confidence will soar—and so will your revenue.

Several intellectual giants have stated, "If you do what you love, you'll never work another day in your life."

That premise is built on passion and purpose, which are the heart and soul of your business. Pinpointing your purpose will energize you to activate the simple, mind-blowing tactics—outlined in this book—to connect you to solid leads and prospective clients, making it easier to sell your services.

Why?

Because you love what you do.

This leads to identifying and developing a profitable, fulfilling business model that allows you to help people *and* do what you love. Building a company with this solid foundation will give you the financial freedom you crave because passion + purpose = profit.

Note: This mindset may produce a desire to profess your deep devotion from the rooftops!

What If You Don't Know What Your Passion Is?

If shining a light on your purpose begins with discovering what you're passionate about, but you're not sure what that is, there are several ways to uncover that information.

Your passion is a dream that has lived inside you, and *only you* can bring it to the surface. If this longing of yours has been buried over time, let's use some compassion and curiosity to seek it out again.

The first step in discovering your passion is to realize it's different for each person. This means *no one* can tell you what you're passionate about when it comes to launching your business. That's for you—and only you—to decide.

Let's Consider An Example: Delicious Dishes

Let me introduce a hypothetical prospect to illustrate how this might work. Suppose you are a chef who has always loved teaching and you've decided to start an innovative cooking school with an attached restaurant that specializes in fusion cooking.

You are thrilled by the idea of creating and teaching a curriculum, but a life cleaning pots, pans, and greasy kitchens doesn't sound appealing. So, once you've created your first test kitchen and café, you decide to leave those details to the chefs (and staff) you will train to start their own schools.

By leveraging your reputation (and, perhaps, your social media following) you build a list of high-end chefs interested in education who are looking for support starting their own schools. The marketing and coursework you're creating will enable them to ramp up quickly in franchising their businesses (school and attached restaurant) under one umbrella—yours.

You call your new business "Delicious Dishes," and your first potential franchisee is Ashley, who also read *The Heart Sell* and is eager to pivot her career. You recently met her at a networking event and have much in common. She shares that she has been overlooked and mistreated by management at the good old boys club.

Having experienced it yourself, you understand the mentality of the male-dominated culture where women are often marginalized, and you schedule your first in-person coffee meeting, making a note to bring your business plan and coursework.

Look For Clues And Answers

Finding your passion involves more than creating a list of strengths and weaknesses, but it's an excellent place to start. (Note: To get the most out of this book, go to dorarankin.com/book-bundle to download worksheets that complement it. Also, designate a journal for notes.)

Let's start by uncovering your passions.

Create two columns with the headers of "Feed Me" and "Abundance." In the "Feed Me" column, list all the things you do to make money now because you have to. In the "Abundance" column, list all the things you've thought about doing but never had the courage to do.

You may find these focus areas challenging, so here's an exercise to help you uncover your calling, your passion, and your purpose. Start by describing at least 15 experiences where you've brought value to the world. (These can be personal, professional, and even painful experiences.) Lean into your life looking for clues and answers about what you've done in the past and what you currently love.

For example, I've been in 12-step recovery for more than half my life, and through that, I've been part of hundreds of experiences that have impacted me and the world around me. This cultivated a theme of helping women who are struggling.

See? It's all inside, but you may have to go looking under some rocks.

Keep digging deeper. Describe the experiences that have brought you to where you are today. What memory burns have made you who you are (good and bad)? Once you've described these life-altering experiences, it's time to share them.

The second part of the exercise in finding your passion is sharing these experiences with a trusted advisor. Choose someone who is open and objective and will listen to you as you weave your way through your discovery. These conversations will provide moments of clarity, and with clarity, your purpose and passion can come to light, and abundance awaits you!

Be Compassionate With Yourself

When working through this exercise, please remember that dislikes and failures are great teaching tools—*if we choose to see them that way.* Over time, your ability to change will help you identify the course your evolution is taking, helping you mark the awareness of your growth. Otherwise, you'll never experience self-discovery, which is where evolution is born.

Some people believe that if you want success, you need to out-fail everyone! Why? Because it's not about perfection. It's about *failing* and *adapting* to discover what works and what you no longer care about. This is an important quality of successful entrepreneurs.

Every time I drive to the airport, I pass by a billboard that has a quote by Abraham Lincoln. It reads, "Failed, failed, failed. And then..." It's an inspirational message about *persistence* and how it leads to success. It reminds me of our ability to endure during hardship, especially when we have passion and purpose behind us.

Remember, not everything in life will be a golden moment of success. We need to embrace opportunities to learn what doesn't work and decide whether to improve something or discard it altogether. For example: *Am I only working on this project to make money, or do I want to keep trying because I'm following my passion?*

The choice is always up to us, though it helps to have a coach who believes in you as you walk through the hard stuff, like failures and flops.

The ability to measure failure and success is one hallmark of a successful business owner.

Finding Your Passion

You may experience a myriad of feelings when taking the wild ride of uncovering your passion and purpose. The one I hear the most is: *What if I fail?*

Why not turn that around? *What if you succeed?*

If you focus on the possibility of failure, your doubts could keep you stagnant. That's why taking action the moment you find clarity is imperative. Clarity without action becomes just another moment that can and will pass. It's time to leap with faith and confidence.

Plant your flag and own it. Use this moment to make a life-changing shift, and allow me to help you with a step-by-step strategy so you can activate your dreams.

Congratulations! You're ready to leap into building your business!

So, now what?

Once your passion is clear, let's dig into your purpose. We'll use my story to help you find yours.

Dora Rankin

CHAPTER 2
Why I Love Helping Women Who Are Struggling

To illustrate why inspiring women to become self-sufficient is so important to me, I'd like to start at the beginning of my story, which includes my favorite role model: my mother, Barbara.

As a single mother with two girls, my mom approached the world around her in a manner that was different from anyone I've ever met. She loved *big*.

As the nursing supervisor who ran a hospital in Warren, Ohio in the eighties and nineties, my powerhouse mother chose a life of service devoted to caring for others. She couldn't help herself; it was rooted in her DNA.

I also admired my mother because she wasn't shy about letting people know how special they were—and I'm not just talking about family and friends. Her patients often asked for her by name, recounting her caring bedside manner, sense of humor, and role in healing them. They valued her ability to shoot from the hip.

Sometimes, she was accused of not having a filter, but people appreciated her honesty.

The Connection Of Two Souls

Thankfully, I've inherited the same style of "telling it like it is." I'm also wired with Mom's over-achieving tendencies, just like my sister, Marcey. Grass doesn't grow under our feet. It's how we roll.

My big sister is five years older than me, and she quickly became Role Model #2 as I watched her create the pattern for everything the "perfect child" represents: kindness, good grades, perfect penmanship, an appreciation for the social graces, and honor-roll level attendance.

I was built differently. There was no way I could compete with that, so I didn't even try. Not overly concerned with personal perfection, I entered my teens as a first-generation latchkey kid who was a bit of a renegade. (In the early eighties, I didn't realize I was paving the way for future batches of single-parent divorcees with teens.)

Buckle Up

When Mom worked overtime running the hospital, and Marcey went away to college, like a typical teen, I decided to find my happiness in creating small adventures and pushing my boundaries.

When I was 13, Mom's youngest would test her love and patience in many unexpected ways. It started when I was offered an opportunity to earn money babysitting a neighbor's children. Everyone knows that one benefit of this type of work involves snooping in the fridge for a yummy snack as the hours pass.

That's what I was doing when *it* happened.

Looking past the sandwich fixings and cheese slices, I found something intriguing tucked away on the lower shelf. It turned a light on in my brain and changed the trajectory of my life.

Is that Kahlua and Cream? How would it work as an ice cream float?

As it turned out, it was delicious. But when I started drinking that day, it started a chain reaction that I couldn't have seen coming. I immediately fell in love with the sense of ease and comfort that went from the top of my head down to my toes. It was heavenly, and I couldn't wait to do it again.

This magic elixir helped me feel unstoppable. I was the life of the party—of one—and because I was so young, I had no idea that I was kicking off what was soon to be the uncontrollable disease of alcoholism.

I had a secret, and no one was the wiser.

Love At First Sip

It seemed to me that alcohol—and all the fixings—was the solution to life, and drinking became my go-to answer for everything. My newly minted concoctions felt like a loyal best friend that accompanied me everywhere I went.

It wasn't long before I was hiding bottles in my school locker and stealing from the local 7-Eleven.

By age 14, I spent most of my waking hours figuring out *where* to locate my next cocktail. When you're a minor and don't have the resources to procure your next drink, you become resourceful, discovering the people and situations that will lead you there.

Consequently, I never turned down a babysitting job, which started with a scavenger hunt the moment the parents left their homes. Doling out the Sunday sacrament during church became a weekly ritual that was an easy go-to as I privately taste-tested the reds in the sanctuary.

Maintaining my growing secret required the cunning reserved for super sleuths, special ops, and enemy spies. I made my mother's life incredibly challenging when I started sneaking out at night or staying out past curfew. She spent several sleepless nights waiting up for me or searching the streets in the dark.

Most of Mom's friends attributed my behavior to typical teenage rebellion, and over time, I found myself lying about where I'd been, who I'd been with, and where the car was—more often than I can remember. Hiding booze in Aqua Net hairspray bottles and showing up hungover at school became part of my daily life.

Tough Love

I spent my teen years perfecting a Dr. Jekyll and Mr. Hyde persona, partying and sneaking around at night while somehow getting to work on time and graduating with a 4.0.

Eventually, right before graduation, my mom found a way to lock me up ... in rehab. She finally got a break, and I got sober for the first time in years.

For a minute, at least.

While I was away, rendezvousing in rehab, my mom found Al-Anon. It saved her sanity and gave her the tools to say "no more" to me when I returned home. This led me to become a homeless, couch-surfing college student.

CHAPTER 3
My Evil Sidekick

After high school, between fraternity parties and hangovers, I started taking classes at Kent State University. Even though my mother was my best friend, I knew I was disappointing her. I didn't understand the disease any more than she did. So, I built a life on secrets and lies to hide my shame, fuel my alcoholism, and look as "normal" as I could, given the circumstances.

For the next year and a half, I couch-surfed, taking advantage of my friends' kindness while working two jobs. The whole thing seemed relatively normal to me. Isn't this what all 18-year-olds do?

At 19, while slipping in and out of blackouts, I met my soon-to-be husband. Before I could drink *legally*, I landed a job in banking, and I got married when I was 21. Who needed school when a future-promised six-figure salary and happy hour consumed my daily life?

That was my routine until I got pregnant, and I managed to stop drinking long enough to have both of my daughters.

Feeling Stuck

As a mother of two, I started managing my first bank branch when I was 23, and that's when the fear of job security kicked in. Desperate to keep my multi-layered lies a secret, I convinced myself that no one knew, which I know today wasn't convincing. I guess we are always the last to know.

There were many mornings filled with hangovers and lots of regrets. I often wondered who suspected, which added a layer of paranoia to the mix. Within two years, I was offered a promotion and was unsure whether I could afford to take it. During that time, I qualified for government assistance, and if I took the promotion, my increased salary meant I would no longer have it.

I had to ask myself if the promotion was worth the cost, financially and emotionally. Today, I see many women stuck in this same dilemma.

Should I or shouldn't I?

I decided to take the promotion, while

realizing I'd have to shoulder the added responsibilities and work harder than the men in my division—just to prove I belonged there.

Playing The Game

I became a successful leader by taking courses in sales training, executive training, leadership coaching, and performance development. Then, I began developing teams to high-achieving levels as well.

My "exceptional performance" was rewarded on stage with cars, trips, bonuses, and huge commission checks. When my name was called in front of hundreds of other bankers at our annual conference, I walked on stage to accept my awards as multi-colored confetti fell on me from the rafters.

It was a surreal moment. Looking back, these enormous gifts and prizes were shallow attempts to motivate me to increase quotas and continue to do as I was told.

There were days (and nights) when I felt like I'd sold my soul to the devil. Most days, when I walked into the bank, I was popping aspirin and chugging coffee, seeking privacy as I leaned my head on the cold steel of the vault, using it as a makeshift compress.

Things Started To Get Real

As I achieved the bank's goals with unyielding energy and enthusiasm, I quickly learned that the following year's goals would be doubled.

Wait. Did I make that look too easy?

This became the pattern at my place of employment. Year after year. It was an untenable expectation, yet upper management continued to insist. I tried to keep any acknowledgment of what I perceived as abuse under wraps with my cover of unyielding enthusiasm. Fear-based thinking powered my performance.

Yes, I was working in a pressure cooker, but I was brainwashed into believing that every high-achieving, top-performing leader worked in that kind of environment. I convinced myself that I needed to keep the job to pay my bills and raise my daughters.

CHAPTER 4
Why Do You Need To Know This About Me?

I'm sharing my background because I want you to know that I understand the struggles women face. I understand feeling stuck in a situation you can't find your way out of. And I also appreciate coming to terms with the fact that you are the problem *and* the solution.

You Can Recover From Whatever's Holding You Back

At age 27, having been married and divorced, with two daughters in my care, I finally got the unmistakable clarity I'd been searching for the day I saw a look of concern from my precious four-year-old, Anna.

After pulling my car over to get sick on the side of the road, Anna asked, "Mommy, are you okay?"

Gazing into her innocent eyes, the look of dread on her face tugged at my heartstrings. Taking a moment to assess what was happening and realizing my behavior was the cause, I drove the rest of the way in silence. It gave me an opportunity for some long-overdue, clear-headed thinking.

Anna's concern was mirrored by Alli's, and she was only two. Before that incident, I made excuses, even though I knew I had a problem. After that, there was no excuse for worrying my daughters as I was.

I'd finally hit rock bottom. It was a sobering moment. That's what finally caught my attention and provided me clarity.

That was the day I asked God for help. It was a huge turning point for me. At the age of 27, after 12 years of denial, it was time to surrender and seek help inside Alcoholics Anonymous.

This is the combination that saved my life.

So, What's The Good News?

Whether you believe it or not, I soon learned that I was good at my job when I was sober, which led me to promotion after promotion, allowing me to complete school and receive titles that 27-year-old women rarely see.

Today, I consider my recovery my "unfair advantage" in my personal and professional successes. What do I mean by that? Learning, in my twenties, that I needed to surrender to something bigger than myself allowed me to let go and seek help, which was incredibly hard for a self-reliant control freak.

Once that was subdued (although I'm a work in progress), I became more relaxed and grateful for the things that *were* working in my life. And every one of the 12 steps helped me get there.

I also believe that if I hadn't gone through those things, I wouldn't be able to support the women I help today. By helping them discover their passion and worth, I've found mine.

I'm genuinely grateful to have found my life's calling while surrounded by people who love me.

Hindsight is a virtue.

I Understand The Struggle

We all have challenges that we need to overcome, and my story shows that I'm no different. As a business mentor and coach, I help entrepreneurs who are lost or feeling stuck get vulnerable and honest about what's holding them back.

I also help them uncover why they stay at jobs that keep them miserable. Most importantly, they discover how to cast off the shackles of corporate imprisonment and doubt while pinpointing their passions.

What's more, the lessons I try to teach aren't just about identifying the excuses that cause women to remain in jobs that are causing misery, just to bring home a paycheck. The same applies to appeasing a spouse, friend, or sibling who bullies you into supporting *their* dreams.

Why? Because right now, this is YOUR moment, and I need you to take some time to luxuriate in the concept of *only thinking about you and your desires*—which I know is a foreign idea to some women (you know who you are).

Most women want to be self-sufficient, but freedom has a different definition for each of us. Now it's your turn. It's time to think about your future and *honor yourself.* (And only yourself.)

Here's The $100,000 Question: What Do You Want?

The simplicity of this question can baffle some, and when I ask my clients this, they often complicate it by sharing their need to please a parent who—for example—has always wanted them to be a lawyer. This is where I want you to ask yourself: *When it comes down to it, do you want to be a lawyer? Or a nurse? Or a restaurant owner? Or are you doing that to please someone else?*

Take a moment, right now. Get your journal and a pen. Close your eyes and imagine what financial freedom would look like for you. Write it down.

Here's the question again, but put differently: *If we only get one chance to live our wild and precious lives, what do you want to do with yours?*

Write it in your journal, now!

It's Time To Be True To Yourself

Maybe you already know how you want to pivot professionally, and if so, that's wonderful! That places you one step ahead of many

others. But let me ask: *If you know exactly what you want to do, why aren't you doing it?*
Why aren't you going after your dreams?

Keep reading. I have some formulas in upcoming chapters that will help.

In the case of our fictitious business called Delicious Dishes, our client Ashley has shared that her biggest fear is leaving her job and paycheck behind. This may also be true for you. (Many things can hold us back.)

For others, your doubts may be quite different. After all, a fear of failure—or success—can be quite natural for some women (as can Imposter Syndrome). Yet, everyone is different, so let's look at what might be holding you back.

CHAPTER 5
You Can't Teach Passion

In chapter one, I asked you to create a two-column list centered around what feeds you and what abundance would be. This exercise helped you discover your passions to pinpoint your purpose. I hope you had fun with it. Now, it's time for a little more frivolity. (You've earned it!)

What would you do if money and prior responsibilities (or obligations) weren't a concern and you could do anything you wanted with your career?

Close your eyes, visualize it, say it out loud:

"If I could do anything, I would _____."

What did you discover? What does it look like? Can you imagine the possibilities?

(At age six, my answer to this question was, "If I could do anything, I'd be a roller-skating cowgirl." Why didn't I fulfill that? Maybe I still can, while empowering you.)

What If It Doesn't Come To You Even After Creating The Lists?

If you read your list but can't decide your passion (and purpose), consider asking the three people closest to you what *they* think you're passionate about. They'll probably tell you exactly what you need to hear, so write it down!

And even though you may end up doing something that few people—or even no one—has attempted before, by combining several items on your list, you'll know you're on the right track when you've fallen in love with your future and feel a jolt of excitement.

Now, ask yourself: *Is this something I know I'm an expert at doing?*

Are you excited about helping people with your particular solution involving the world of _____ (fill in the blank: finance, writing, design, accounting, architecture, social media, etc.).

You Are Extraordinary

When you've found your match, realize that it may evolve into something completely different over time, and that's okay. Right now, we're taking baby steps to get you going in the right direction.

If, on the other hand, you *aren't* excited about the options you've listed, you need to dig deeper. If there's one thing professional coaches around the world agree upon, it's that *you can't teach passion.*

As you dig deeper, I want you to remember that what comes naturally to you might seem *extraordinary* to others. Your passion might be right in front of you; you just don't know it yet.

This means that you're either crazy in love with the idea of dedicating your life to something, or you're not. That's why *only you* can choose what you're passionate about—no one else can.

As you consider your future, consider this quote from Rumi, a 13th-century poet:

It's your road and yours alone. Others may walk it with you, but no one can walk it for you.

An Extended Family

After the incident with my daughters, I took a long, hard look at myself and didn't like what

I saw. I got busy in AA and became sober on June 6, 2004, at the age of 27. I found an "old school" sponsor and did as I was told, which was a new experience for me. Attending meetings most days of the week, I lugged my daughters with me, and the attendees and organizers always welcomed us. Church basements became my new home.

Surrounding myself with loving strangers who understood the trials and tribulations of alcoholism was the best decision I could have made. For several years, my daughters (and I) grew up with that extended family, and we still do.

Two decades later, I realize AA has humbled me into happiness, and I'll be forever grateful.

Juggling

Six months after I became sober, my mother came to live with me. She fell and never got back up after being diagnosed with Multiple Sclerosis (M.S.). As a result, my 47-year-old mother lost the ability to walk, becoming paralyzed from the waist down and needing 24-hour care.

Although her doctors presented me with several options, including assisted living and at-home professional care, I decided she would live with us. So, I had our home completely renovated to become wheelchair-friendly, with ramps and a first-floor bedroom, to make things easy for her.

After she moved in, the girls and I quickly adapted to a new lifestyle centered around caring for my mother; even my eight-year-old daughter learned to change catheters.

This ushered in one of the most challenging times of my life, with responsibilities on all fronts. Along with a stress-filled job, where I constantly had to prove (and outdo myself), I worried about my girls and my sick mother.

Looking back now, I don't know how I did it all. Several times, we had to call the fire department (I had them on speed dial) because Mom would fall and the girls and I couldn't lift her off the floor by ourselves.

The End Of My Rope

After Mom moved in, I remember crying a lot when no one else was around. I felt trapped in my roles as caregiver, mother, and high-pressure bank executive. Then, at an AA meeting, I heard about a conference in Columbus that I wanted to attend.

But feelings of guilt loomed large. I couldn't

leave my family alone, could I? The thought of attending the conference kept haunting me, and I can't explain it, but I felt that there might be someone there who could help.

After much deliberation, I scheduled some at-home care for Mom and left for the event. When I arrived, I couldn't relax and enjoy myself. Instead, I bent the ear of anyone who would listen, hoping someone, somewhere, could help.

I was at another emotional rock bottom, filled with rage and a desperate feeling of abandonment.

I remember being in the ladies' room and telling a friend that I just wanted *someone* to come in and fix things for me. I wanted to run away from the high-stress, hire-wire act that was my life.

I told her, "It's been six years of this, and I don't want to care for a sick mother anymore. I want a different life!"

Twenty minutes later, I told another friend the same thing, asking her, "What are my options? These are the cards I've been dealt."

I received a lot of sympathy but not a lot of help.

Most of my peers, who were 30 and 40-somethings, had never been in my situation, so they didn't have the experience to offer any help.

The Tides Shifted

During the weekend, I had the good fortune of hearing a story of hope from someone who would later turn out to be my angel. Mari shared her experience, strength, and the hope she found through sobriety, catching my attention when she talked about the five years she spent caregiving for her ex-husband.

She spoke about how those years were bittersweet, a combination of being some of the most challenging of her life while also providing the biggest blessing she had ever received in her new sobriety.

I had to understand how she survived it.

Is This A Sign?

Mari's story enthralled me, so after her lead (jargon we use in AA), I ran up to the podium and introduced myself.

I said, "Mari, my name is Dora. When you were talking about caring for your ex-husband, it really spoke to me. I'm finding myself in a similar situation with my ailing mother. I'm feeling so filled with frustration—and desperation—right now."

As I explained the details of my life, she nodded intently.

"There are days when I feel like I just can't do it anymore," I added, "and I want to run away and escape from all the responsibilities. Please help me understand what to do."

She grabbed me by the chin and said, "Honey, trust me when I tell you that you will know love as you've never known it before."

I just looked at her.

As she gathered her things, she said, "Hindsight is a virtue. Just hold on. You're doing a great job with your mom and your family. You'll get through this, I promise."

Then she winked and walked away.

Now I Get It

Years later, after my mother passed away, I remembered the moment I shared with Mari at the conference—and, as it turns out, she was right. I realized that by loving my mother with all my heart, making her care my priority, and comforting her as she'd once cared for me, I received the biggest blessing I'd ever experienced: I'd known love as I'd never known it before.

I also understood that it wasn't something I could appreciate when I was in the middle of it, when the long road ahead only showed more of the same. It was something I could only appreciate through hindsight, knowing I did everything I could for her.

I also have to admit that caring for Mom when she needed me most was my chance to make amends for all the things I'd put her through during my years of active alcoholism when I didn't come home for days and worried her half to death.

Looking back, I'm humbled by the experience because hindsight *is* a virtue. I never need to feel bad about anything relating to my mother because I gave her my all—and I'd do it again in a heartbeat.

Mom Was On A Mission

I have to add one more thing regarding the story of my mother. Before she died, the most important thing to her was finding someone to care for me. She often said, "I don't want to die and leave you all alone."

At the time, I was dating a remarkable man, so I took the liberty of assuring her that John was "the one"—even though I had no idea if I would marry him. (I announced it to her impulsively—we'd only been dating for four months!)

That conversation seemed to give her a sense of peace at a time when pain and fear were taking up most of the little energy she had left. It was a bittersweet time for me because my mother was terminally ill, but I was falling in love for the first time in over a decade.

Two years after Mom died, I married my husband, John, who is a wonderful man. It's not lost on me that the timing was tragic in one sense, yet magical in another. Yes, I had a lot to deal with during my first years of sobriety. But because I was on the road to cleaning up my life *before* Mom moved in, I was better prepared to deal with the next decade of caring for her.

Today, I'm happy to say that I am also surrounded by two healthy, happy daughters, good friends, and a community of women who soar.

We do it together.

The Heart Sell

Dora Rankin

Section Two
Championing Women

Dora Rankin

CHAPTER 6
The Hard Sell Vs. The Heart Sell

What if I told you that the power of financial freedom is within your reach? My clients and I have repeatedly proven that shifting our thinking is the first step to gaining financial freedom. And with that comes personal excellence and self-reliance.

Stop Assuming And Start Heart Selling

We all know the difference between meeting a pushy salesman (yuck) versus someone showing sincere interest in you with the ability to solve a problem. This is the difference between the "hard sell" and The Heart Sell.

Which do you prefer?

That's part of the shift.

Leading with your heart is the best way to show up in the world. When you're eager to help people solve their problems, it shows.

Lead By Example

In chapter one, I shared a short definition of The Heart Sell, but in this chapter, I will cover why I call it that and *how it will benefit you.*

During my tenure at the bank, I was fortunate to have another great mentor. Jane was the president of retail banking, and she loved to champion women. She taught me about the power of morning "huddles," and I quickly learned this was a powerful tactic for getting to know, like, and trust my boss and the other members of our team.

I studied her management style as she helped us grow into our careers while nurturing her relationship with each of us. She often stated that "there's no substitute for human connection."

When I became a leader, I instituted her practices with my team, even though her tactics were contrary to popular management styles. Fortunately, over the years, I pulled together great teams that also felt comfortable enough to tell it like it is. They often described me as a mix of sincere, yet bossy. Someone even included my favorite descriptor: stubborn.

That made me laugh because it sounded like

they were talking about my best friend—my mother!

Office Buzz

Because I don't filter my comments, my crew knew I would be compassionate with any problem they had — professionally or personally — and they could also rely on me to be super transparent.

For example, if someone on my team was having difficulty with a customer, I listened to them, took a beat, and gave them my complete attention, lifting them up instead of tearing them down. This latchkey kid never wanted anyone to feel alone or neglected.

Next, I would coach them, like I do with my clients today. In most cases, each individual chose their own solution, which they ran by me before taking action. Because of the level of trust we shared, we could often circumvent a problem before it happened.

This method yielded fantastic benefits as our team started surpassing others at work, meeting and exceeding our yearly goals. (Free cars, trips, and bonuses, remember?) Several competitive male colleagues began watching me closely while questioning my management style.

There was a buzz throughout the office. *What is Dora doing differently, and how can I get in on the action?*

I Began To Wonder

Unfortunately, as I continued to move up the ranks, I didn't report to leaders with the same management style as mine, and the contrast was *stark*. One day, as I walked away from a meeting, I mumbled while comparing our different management techniques.

I heard myself say, "It's management by intimidation vs. leading from the heart—*selling from the heart.*"

That's when the term "heart sell" was born—in my mind. I kept the concept to myself for years as I continued to nurture my crew. Since I knew managing from a place of love or compassion was something few men would appreciate, I didn't share it for fear of ridicule.

It was my very own "secret sauce."

I Felt Powerful And In Control

Over time, I was recruited to other banks and quickly became a regional sales director. Eagerly sharing everything I'd learned from past employers with my new team, I quickly realized that I learned as much—if not more—from them as they learned from me.

Because people sought my advice regarding their ambitious goals, by the time I was 30, I was promoted to the position of vice president and was treated like a freaking rock star. As the pressure mounted, I became extremely anxious as I continued my climb.

I convinced myself that I could handle everything coming at me because, after all, look at the results I'd produced!

Let Me Ask You This ...

Are you currently working in what feels like a pressure cooker? Is your boss constantly heaping more pressure on you because you've risen to the challenge in the past? Do you have crazy deadlines, insufferable conditions, or inconsiderate colleagues?

Now that I'm out of the corporate atmosphere, I realize how *unsafe and unhealthy* I felt when I was working there—but I never could have articulated it at the time.

Why? Because I thought my job brought financial security. But it was just a façade.

After working for 17 years at different financial institutions, I learned to play the game no matter who my boss was. Most of us do it to survive the political office culture. Over time, we slowly adapt to corporate environments while trying to fly under the radar and keep our heads down.

A New Routine

Eventually, things got so bad that I had *another* secret: Every morning on my drive to work, I was experiencing gut-wrenching panic attacks—for the first time in my life. This new routine lasted almost three years, starting a year after my mother passed, causing me to stop on the side of the road to get sick and compose myself.

In anxiety-ridden phone calls with my sister, Marcey, I kept asking, "How can I do better than 'exceptional?'"

I visited my doctor and got on the right medication to handle these episodes, and I started feeling better. But the panic attacks didn't stop until after I left the banking industry.

I Was A Chameleon

Looking back, I'm stunned at my ability to morph my personality into becoming whatever my employer needed me to be on any given day. Should I work faster? Slower? Be more feminine? Assertive? More humorous? More serious?

It was a confusing and demeaning environment. I was expected to redefine myself with chameleon-like skills at every boardroom meeting, performance review, and client appointment. And it was all done for the long-awaited pat on the back.

The problem was that I wasn't being true to myself, so I was miserable. I didn't realize it then, but I was living a lie, and it was finally catching up with me.

I said a prayer. It was answered.

Having Faith

As it turns out, being fired was one of the best things that ever happened to me (goodbye indentured servitude!) because no matter how miserable I was, I wouldn't have done it on my own. My fear was so great that, as I walked out of those bank doors for the last time, I honestly believed I'd be homeless within a month.

After being given my walking papers, I spent the next three months decompressing by painting every room in my house. It was a prism of rainbow colors that allowed me to change my thought patterns and clear my head.

After the fog lifted, I spoke to my grandpa, our family's patriarch, about my fears.

He said, "Dora, you may have been feisty in your teens, but in the grand scheme of things—when you had to—you took good care of your girls and your mom. That's why I believe you can do anything you want.

"Keep an open mind, dear. When I graduated from Cornell, I never guessed that my career would lead me the way it did. You're a smart, independent woman, and you can do whatever you set your mind to. Have you thought about giving school another whirl? Maybe a new major or certification could lead you into the new direction you're seeking."

I shrugged my shoulders.

He hesitated for a moment and said, "I'm going to give you some grand advice that my father gave me. Just remember this: When you control your money, you control your life." I thought about that. Grandpa was always led by his strong faith, and I respected that.

After talking to him, I felt better.

Later, I thought about his alma mater, Cornell University, and how he always spoke highly of it. As I Googled it online, I scrolled through all the certification courses, and the one that jumped out at me was Empowering Women's Leadership.

I immediately signed up, and not long after, I started looking around for opportunities.

Time For A Change

In 2018, while at Cornell, I started working for a high-growth fintech (financial/technology) start-up specializing in crowdfunding backed by VC (venture capital) investment partners. This is an area where few women tread, let alone lead.

My job was to activate the market by getting people to buy our product, which no one had heard of. Ultimately, our goal was to get money into the right hands while helping people the banks were overlooking: women and other minorities.

Our mission was so exciting!

But after three years, my expectations were slowly deteriorating. And when I attended our industry convention in 2020, there were only *three women* in a sea of hundreds of (mostly white) men.

When I complained to my male colleagues about the ratio, one nodded his head and quipped that I should feel "lucky" or "honored" to be one of the chosen. That's when I sadly realized inclusion was not their primary goal.

Deep in my heart, I knew the tech startup wasn't the right fit either. After that, I became disenchanted with the job and tendered my resignation.

CHAPTER 7

Have You Ever Felt Lost?

For my 43rd birthday, Marcey and I continued the tradition of celebrating by meeting for the weekend at the halfway point between Cleveland and Kentucky. Because Mom's birthday was close to mine, we always included her by sharing loving memories and making a toast in her honor.

Over Peanut Buster Parfaits, I said, "I've decided that I don't want to work at the startup anymore, and I certainly don't want to work for another bank. I'm feeling a little lost."

Marcey put her DQ down. "Dora, you've helped a lot of CEOs and businesses make a *ton of money* over the years! Why don't you take everything that's wrapped around your pinky finger and help women business owners? You're the golden goose! If you can do it for others, why not yourself?"

With a mouth full of ice cream, I smiled. I let that sink in.

Then I pointed to myself. "Wait! Me? I never thought about running my own business. I only build others."

"Hold on," Marcey pointed out. "You ran an entire bank, working alongside CEOs to help them build their net growth. You did this all while developing leaders to their maximum potential, raising two daughters, and taking care of Mom. You've got this!"

I smiled.

"Not to mention you recently worked inside a start-up, building it for the last three years," she added. "Everyone has counted on you to hit all the goals like a freaking pinball machine. Bing, bing, bing! And then they threw more and more at you, and you met those goals too!"

"Until I cracked!" I said with a laugh.

"C'mon!" she encouraged. "If you can do that, certainly you can start your own business!"

I thought about that. "Well, what would that look like? Where would I start?"

"We'll figure that out later. You've had career personality tests, and they showed that your strengths are 'creating strategies,' followed by 'execution' and 'bringing people together.'

"That's the foundation of any good business owner. Plus, you know how to make mega bucks for the banks, so why not teach people how to do that? Maybe you can create a business that helps women soar?"

As I took in everything she was saying, I was speechless. My mind was whirling at 100 miles per hour and my heart was beating fast.

"Dora, are you considering this?"

That was one of the few times in my life when I had total clarity.

I nodded. "Yes!"

It was like my big sister had given me permission to do something I wouldn't have considered on my own. As we exchanged high fives, I knew it was a huge turning point.

I owe Marcey a debt of gratitude.

Coaching Vs. Consulting

A month later, I hired a business coach who taught me the difference between a consultant and a coach.

A consultant is an expert who advises you on decision-making and overall guidance. A coach asks a series of questions to help the client solve their own problems. They often address issues such as fear, limiting beliefs, mindset, and self-confidence.

I often recommend hiring a business coach because if you're stuck in a situation and can't discover the problem—let alone the solution—a series of thought-provoking questions can clear out the cobwebs. (You don't have to hire me, but having a good one-on-one coach can be life-changing.)

This exercise will help walk you through the bottlenecks in your business and the reasons for them. Then, someday, when the coach isn't there, you can revisit the questions that launched your discovery to find a solution before going off course.

You Have Options!

Within weeks of starting my business, I took on my first client, scheduling six months of coaching as I imparted my experience working with banks, business owners, and start-ups.

One of the many things I love about coaching clients who are serious about doing the hard work necessary to make powerful changes is that those changes can happen rather quickly. Sometimes, it takes a little handholding to walk someone through the steps—and that's okay. Everyone works at their own pace.

When my first client's business started receiving a boost, so did my confidence. Once she was off and running, I took on my second, third, and fourth clients while discovering my specialty areas and raising my rates (which you will be doing, too!).

I love what I do, and I've discovered that helping people find their purpose and grow their wealth also allows them to discover their personal freedoms.

Stuck In No-Win Situations

When people inquire about working with me as their business coach, they often choose to start our working relationship *after* they've left the doctrines of corporate America and the "fog" has lifted.

I once heard of a company that liked to hire people based on the results of a personality test that proved the candidate had a high level of responsibility combined with low self-esteem. Why? Having complete access to someone who constantly needs to prove they're worthy makes for a heck of a workhorse.

They Have An Agenda

Looking back to my corporate career, I was almost 30 years old when I was promoted to vice president of commercial lending and business banking. I managed teams, billion-dollar budgets, and multi-million-dollar branches.

I was brainwashed into believing that my life needed to revolve around bringing more cash into the bank, but the problem was, no matter how many boxes I checked, they kept moving the goalpost. If I didn't meet my weekly goals, I had to show up at 7:00 a.m. to tell them why.

It was embarrassing, humiliating, and exhausting. But that was the point.

I felt like I was trapped in a no-win situation in a prison-like setting, with the warden and guards constantly hammering me about achieving *more*.

Whatever It Takes

Sometimes, the women I work with also need to seek counseling, which I understand, because the employer-employee relationship can be akin to selling oneself for a weekly paycheck—what I call "corporate trafficking."

It's grooming and brainwashing.

Although I'm sure there are great employers to work for where this isn't the case, generally speaking, working for "the man" comes at a price. On one hand, it's good training for starting your own company because you receive a valuable education in business on someone else's dime.

On the other hand, we agree to give up certain rights on day one and may even sign a contract to that effect. Meanwhile, we overlook the increasing microaggressions and expectations shoveled on us over time.

It's subtle and suffocating.

Stay tuned: We will get down to business—yours—to help you discover your audience and target market and the best ways to grow your business. I'll also define the difference between marketing and sales and how that differentiation is important to your bottom line.

Dora Rankin

Section Three
Building Relationships

Dora Rankin

CHAPTER 8
Find Your Audience

There is currently an epidemic of women leaving corporate America to start their own businesses. I find this wave exciting as I think of Grandpa's words: *When you control your money, you control your life.*

Over the years, I've heard from many women who tell me they've done "everything they're supposed to do," but they're *struggling* to earn a living wage. No one taught them how to build a business; they've only been taught how to sell a course, a product, or a service online.

They're missing the best part: a growth strategy centered around relationships!

Fast forward several months or years from the inception of their businesses, and they're barely making it week to week. By the time they call me, their desperation is palpable, and consequently, our first meetings can be rather intense. But I understand their concerns—and I have a winning formula!

In our first meeting, in alignment with everything you've read so far, I ask these women several questions to ensure their passion aligns with their purpose. That's always the first step. The next step in building financial freedom is building relationships.

Or, as my big-hearted mother would say, "People make the world go round."

Your Perfect Client

When I talk to my clients, their biggest concerns revolve around not knowing how or where to find their clients.

Does this sound familiar?

To discover your perfect client/customer, start with an audience audit by answering these questions:

- Who needs your products/services (or the solutions they solve)? No one should know that better than you!
- Is there an individual or business that needs what you are selling?
- Is there a product/service people want that no one else is fulfilling?

If you don't know the answer to that last question, talk to people in your industry to discover where the "holes" are in the marketplace. Then, consider the best ways to fill them.

Make an exhaustive list. You can always pare it down later. There's no such thing as having too many leads. Finding your target market will take research and ingenuity, but once you've established your best client/customer, it's just a matter of reaching out to them with the solutions you provide with The Heart Sell.

Your target audience is the driver of all your revenue-generating activities. It's the first "Q" of the formula Q x Q = R (a Quality audience x Quantity/Volume = Results).

Refining Your Audience

Once you've decided who your customer is, the next thing you need to consider is whether your products and services are suitable for individuals, as in "business to consumer" (B2C), or other companies, as in "business to business" (B2B). Identifying which of these is your best client/customer is essential because if you go after the wrong client, you can spin your wheels for years—without knowing it.

I see it all the time!

Audience Audit

My Ideal Client Qualifiers	
Company _____	Position _____
Industry _____	Income/Revenue _____
Location _____	Company Size _____
Interests _____	
Influenced by _____	

What problem do you solve that your ideal client already knows that they have?	**What problem do you solve** that your ideal client <u>does not know</u> that they have?

Partners: Who serves your ideal client, but solves a different problem than you?	**Ecosystem:** Where does your ideal client hang out as part of a group—with peers?

For example, I had a client who left corporate America to become a freelance writer. She targeted corporations and ad agencies (B2B) because they had big budgets and big projects.

But several years into it, she was mired in the old familiar red tape of working with corporations, remembering how it slowed everything down, including her pay. So, she focused on coaching other writers (B2C) and loved her clients' immediate feedback (and payment).

Once you've answered the questions of who needs your products/services (your target market) and which type of customer you will focus on (B2B or B2C), you've achieved the first two critical steps in finding leads and creating revenue.

Next, we'll get you started on creating leads.

The Importance Of Know + Like + Trust

In the business world, there is a saying that rises above all others: *People do business with people they know, like, and trust.* Earning your client's trust is the goal because when people trust you, they respect you and feel comfortable referring you and/or doing business with you.

Develop A Sales Strategy

In my 25 years of experience building and leading sales teams and advising women in business, I have found that very few people understand what a sales strategy is, which can make it impossible to implement!

It's All About "Lead Generation"

One of the easiest and most consistent ways to generate sales leads is to *always* have three working lists marked "Hot," "Warm," or "Cold."

Hot Leads. Create a list of hot leads or close connections. These are the people who meet at the intersection of already knowing, liking, and trusting you while needing your services to enhance their businesses or projects. Some may be industry colleagues and friends, others may be acquaintances you see regularly at church or sporting events. This is your most important list. You should always have five to ten people on your hot list.

Warm Leads. This list will include warm leads from other acquaintances, including people you've met at seminars, conferences, or for coffee in the past year. They know you and may even like you. Meeting with them again will help them get to know you and your business as you continue to build trust. Soon, you will feel comfortable offering them leads, and some will return the favor.

These two lists are where you want to start your search for leads.

Cold Leads. This list will be your cold leads—people you do not know—compiled from research of companies and individuals connected to industries that need your product/service. You can experiment with various lead database software programs and test them to discover which best suits your needs.

Creating a high-quality prospect list may take time and effort, but it will pay off when you realize who your competition is, who your prospects are, and where you can find them. Keep in mind, these lists will need to be updated regularly, so schedule time to data mine and optimize your list.

The Goal Is Building Relationships!

The goal of every industry event, face-to-face meeting, or online conversation is to continue building good relationships that will allow people to get to know, like, and trust you.

Then—and only then—can you walk them down the path to see if there's an opportunity to solve their problem, maybe even a problem they don't know they have. This is called The Heart Sell conversation.

That's it. That's the whole goal.

Suppose it ends in a sale. That's great. If it doesn't, it might conclude with a referral to another company. And that would only come from someone who trusts you and the solutions you offer.

That's another way the *Know, Like, and Trust Principle* works.

What Not To Do

Because I've been doing this for so long, I know what can kickstart a great sales process or drown out a bad one.

Let's start with a list of the things I *don't* want you to do:

- I don't want you playing the numbers game and cold-calling a bunch of people with knots in your stomach.
- I don't want you digging through social media for prospects and sending DMs that make you want to hide under the covers before (or after) you hit send.

- I don't want you pitching your products or services unless you are 100% certain you can help someone and they are ready to invest in solving a problem.

Here is what I want you to concentrate on instead:

- I want you to build relationships. That's it!

In other words, stop waiting for people to find you and *start finding your people*—in a way that feels good to you! Learn to love, and lead with, non-salesy sales calls.

In case you didn't know, Sara Blakely, the founder of Spanx, was so passionate about her product that she wore her Spanx shirt for an entire year while building relationships with her buyers. She used The Heart Sell without even knowing it! Relationship building, leading with service, and getting to know your buyer makes both of you more comfortable.

Dora Rankin

CHAPTER 9
The Key To Your Heart

❤———————————————❤

I want you to find the definition of sales that allows you to fall in love with it. My definition is: Love your business and the work you develop with your clients.

Get Leads Using The Heart Sell's 80/20 Rule

The 80/20 Rule offers offline person-to-person growth strategies that can be used in conjunction with your online strategies to help you scale your business. It states that you should spend 80% of your time developing growth strategies through outbound relationship selling activities and 20% on inbound marketing. Building relationships as your business' core strategy will help you attract and retain clients, and using the 80/20 Rule is a game changer!

Time + Commitment = Power

In this online, data-driven world, there is a strategic, four-step process to create leads that convert into consistent revenue using a plan that includes weekly outreach, partnerships, ecosystems, and marketing.

1. Outreach. Through outreach, you'll experiment with discovering who your target audience is and reaching out to them directly. Once you go through the audience audit exercise, you'll gain more understanding of your target audience so you can develop a strategic plan around your outreach. You needn't be overwhelmed with your outreach strategy. This is your opportunity to narrow your choices down to discover who your buyers are and where they hang out. (The Heart Sell course teaches you exactly how to do this. Go to dorarankin.com for more details.)

2. Partnerships. The best partnerships include developing strategic relationships with people who have the same audience as you but do something completely different. The more you proactively foster these relationships, the more mutual benefits you'll see. The goal is to refer customers to each other regularly. As a banker, the perfect non-competitive alliances for me were accountants because we both offered different services within the financial industry. (This is one-to-one relationship building.)

3. Ecosystems. Define the organizations that have your audience—in masses—and need your support. Cast a wide net as the expert in your area of interest so everyone knows you for that product/service. Attend events at different companies, conferences, and organizations and get to know people. This one takes the most time and energy but can produce the best results. (This is one-to-many relationship/partnership building.)

4. Inbound Marketing. Marketing will create credibility and nurture your sales strategy; it's not meant to increase sales.

Your biggest aha! moment is knowing *what* to prioritize and *when*. Back to the 80/20 Rule: Marketing is how your people find you, and sales is how you find your people. Revenue comes from your weekly *outreach*, not from your marketing. That's the difference.

You now have a weekly plan of action that gets you into the world with that big heart of yours so you can share the solutions your products/services offer.

When Sales And Marketing Work Together

One of my favorite examples of a business successfully executing a sales and marketing strategy is the Little Words Project. The founder, Adriana Carrig, began designing and creating bracelets in her home and her family led the sales strategy by selling her jewelry at farmers' markets throughout her local area. Her parents helped her make the bracelets and her husband worked on the business operations.

For several years, Adriana stole the show at local events by sharing how important building relationships can be. Soon, she landed a contract with 700 Nordstrom stores, and in 2023, she went viral on the MTV Video Music Awards when Taylor Swift gave the project a shout-out as she accepted her award.

Do you see the connection?

Marketing wasn't the driver. Her bracelets went viral because of the relationships she built.

Icebreakers

If you're an introvert, you may wonder how to start engaging in conversations with prospective clients or even "strangers" in group meetings or events. If that's you, I have great news. One of the best ways to start building relationships is by sincerely sharing common interests.

Some people do this so naturally that they don't even realize they're doing it. Think about the last time you complimented a stranger on her new earrings, homemade salsa dip, or choice of continuing education class. You created a conversation starter that began with a common interest. (It's a great icebreaker!) That's a great start, but let's go further.

Nurture Those Contacts

Building your business takes work. At times, you'll need to commit to relentless effort—especially in the beginning—to get up to speed and gain momentum. But if you are building it while rooted in your purpose, you will love nurturing it and watching it grow!

You could say it's the key to your heart.

Once you have a weekly plan that results in consistent conversations with your target audience, partners, and ecosystem, things become much easier because you've built a growth strategy centered on revenue-generating activities. This win-win is important to nurture, and there are different ways to do this that include anything from sending leads to other alliances to scheduling "coffee calls" without leaving your desk.

An Example Of Where A Relationship Can Take You

Using our Delicious Dishes example, let me illustrate how a simple conversation and relationship can help bring profits into your business. Remember, this example positions you as starting a fusion cooking school with an adjacent test kitchen/restaurant under the Delicious Dishes franchise umbrella.

After doing your research, you realize there's a gap in the marketplace. No one else in your community (within 500 square miles) is training other high-end chefs to become teachers in their own cooking schools. This is a huge opportunity to start your business locally!

We mentioned that you met with Ashley (your potential B2B franchise client), and through your early conversations, you find she knows several chefs who want to start their own schools. In the case of a warm lead like Ashley, she already knows and likes you, so you've already achieved two-thirds of the Know + Like + Trust equation.

Because you also want to earn her trust, you're transparent in answering her questions while encouraging and valuing her input. Trust and respect go hand in hand.

After asking and considering pertinent questions about what she wants for her cooking school, you discover she's passionate about creating an after-school program for teenagers who like to bake. You listen and take notes.

Then, the two of you formulate a plan that also includes *your* goals. You're passionate about having the schools cross-promote the restaurants with "best of" menus and taste-testing challenges.

As you develop your plan, Ashley creates some brochures and visits area high schools to promote her after-school bake-offs (with samples, of course!). Meanwhile, you create an online campaign asking the public to visit the restaurants and vote for their favorite meals, which you will highlight on social media. As you agree to promote each other's marketing efforts, a win-win strategy is born.

The Importance Of Partnerships And Ecosystems

At your next meeting with Ashley, you ask her to create her three lists. As she does, she circles two names, including someone named Frank at the top of her hot list. She mentions that they've been trying to schedule a meeting to explore ideas.

When you sit down with them, they discuss starting a franchised school/restaurant—as partners—on the opposite side of town.

Frank is excited and shares that he has good relationships with local food service providers and a cookware company that would be interested in cross-promotional partnerships. He also mentions that his brother, Hank, is starting a cooking show challenge on TikTok.

Ashley suggests having chefs from Delicious Dishes as contestants. Frank nods enthusiastically, saying Hank had suggested the same thing!

You realize how this kind of coverage—and these two connections—could provide you with more opportunities for success than doing it alone. To test the market, the three of you decide to create pop-ups in different cities to see if the concept is well received. The following week, you're inundated with requests and realize it's time to open the first two schools.

Congratulations! You have two hot leads for your cooking school, and the launch of Delicious Dishes is on its way!

Keep Going

As a business owner—you should always be working to develop your three lead lists because even if your calendar is full of client projects and meetings, you want to continue building your lead pipeline so that when potential clients fall off the list, there are several others to meet with.

With your strategy taking shape, you and Ashley decide that one of you should go to New York City to attend an annual cooking conference to find warm leads. Ashley offers to go, and you decide to attend several local networking events and conduct research on a company that specializes in helping franchised businesses enter the market.

You've just learned the four ways to earn consistent revenue using the 80/20 Rule (Outreach/Sales vs. Online Marketing), how to use sincere icebreakers while nurturing your contacts, and how to create a pipeline of leads that can be converted into sales using a simple strategy. That should keep your cash register humming.

Like a boss!

Dora Rankin

CHAPTER 10
Consider a "Sales First" Approach

In today's world, digital marketing can seem like the only way to grow your business. Because of that, you may have already invested thousands into websites, programs, and courses that have taught you how to build an online business and "watch it grow while you sleep."

However, understanding the difference between marketing and sales will be the key to rapidly building your business and even flourishing as an entrepreneur. The truth is, you don't need digital marketing *or* social media to grow your business.

Let me repeat that: You don't need digital marketing *or* social media to build your business.

Why not?

Because, as a woman, your ability to lead from

the heart, while building valuable relationships, is more valuable than you know.

Why A Mindset Shift Is Critical To Growing Your Business

Let's return to the fundamentals of business before the Internet unleashed the "build-it-and-they-will-come" mentality (regarding online content). Ask yourself this: How did so many companies become so successful before the invention of the online world?

They had two (offline) teams focused solely on growth: a marketing team *and* a sales team. And they still do!

Even today, the most lucrative Fortune 500 businesses, VC-backed high-growth startups, and solopreneur endeavors have marketing *and* sales teams focused on growing revenue.

Why Is Online Marketing Promoted As The Answer?

First, let me say I'm *not* anti-online marketing; heck, I write blogs about best practices. However, to grow your business, you must uncover the best way to reach prospective customers and develop an *integrated* strategy with (inbound) marketing and (outbound) sales.

Let's look at both sides of the coin. Marketing campaigns include your website, newsletters, direct mail, billboards, social media postings, ads, SEO, and blogs, to name a few. In all cases, content is created and dispersed through different channels, requiring people to find you. This is a great way to test your audience and see who responds. I like to call this the inbound approach.

Marketing is *not* your sales process. Its primary role is to nurture your sales process and add credibility. The truth is, marketing isn't directly connected to revenue like we think it is.

Sales are directly connected to your revenue, and making this shift in mindset will give you more control over your bottom line, allowing you to increase your earnings more quickly!

For Faster Results, Use A "Sales First" Approach

Marketing is a long game, often taking *12-18 months* to see consistent results. Because of this, you can become exhausted trying to keep up with different tactics, not knowing where your customers/clients are coming from, which makes it difficult to find more.

On the other hand, if you want to stop the

revenue rollercoaster, you need to develop a strategic process that prioritizes sales, which is directly connected to increasing your revenue. Once you learn this skillset, you can create a steady flow of quality leads in *three to six months.*

If marketing is a marathon, sales is a 100-meter race.

How does that sound?

Let's Compare The Two

If marketing is how your people find you, then sales is how *you* find your people. With marketing, you invest time and energy creating content only to hope the right people will find you. But we lean too heavily on marketing because it feels safe.

Sales is *proactive* and high-touch with one-on-one or in-person outreach. Yes, there's a process to it, but it's a formula for success.

As I mentioned earlier, the parent formula for every sales activity is Q x Q = R (Quality of audience x Quantity and volume = Results.) We'll dig into your quality audience and quantity (list building) shortly.

Sales vs. Marketing

SALES ↓	MARKETING ↓
HOW YOU FIND YOUR CLIENTS	HOW YOUR CLIENTS FIND YOU
PROACTIVE	REACTIVE
OUTBOUND	INBOUND
NURTURES YOUR BOTTOM LINE	NURTURES YOUR SALES PROCESS
3-6 MONTH RUNWAY	12-18 MONTH+ RUNWAY
RELATIONSHIP DRIVEN	METRICS AND DATA DRIVEN

It's All About Mindset

The word "sales" gets a bad rap.

I want you to think about every job interview you've ever had. As you sat across from the recruiter, did you realize you were "selling" your talent, time, and energy to a company looking for your skillset?

Maybe you didn't realize it then, but you were in sales mode, hoping to get the job. Some will argue that we're selling all the time! Whether you want to persuade your in-laws to let you host the next Thanksgiving dinner or convince your son's little league coach to let little Russell play in the next game, you're selling an idea. But, in both cases, you're selling from the heart, so it feels *easier.*

Right?

Because women naturally lead from the heart, people are drawn to us and we make friends easily. Then, adding in our natural tendencies for compassion and nurturing those we love, many of our relationships last decades.

Putting that passion into our businesses and selling from the heart is a natural progression for women business owners. The Heart Sell turns the Hard Sell on its head, which is why providing a unique service will be an easy sell for you.

More Proof

A colleague once told me that she sought the advice of a career placement specialist after a layoff when considering whether to return to the workforce or start her own business.

The career placement specialist told her, "If you're considering business ownership, I hope you're comfortable with the idea of selling because, as an entrepreneur, you'll be selling every day for the rest of your life."

She thought about that for a moment as the realization hit her hard.

Then he added, "But you'll also become a leader—an expert—regarding the unique product or service you offer."

Was she ready for that?

In her case, the answer was yes because she'd done her time in corporate America.

There was no turning back. She was ready to be free.

Soon after, she learned the concept behind The Heart Sell, and she consistently increased her revenue with an integrated strategy that included in-person outreach and one-on-one meetings.

Even if *you* are your sales team, you must include outreach if you want your business to flourish. That's why I want you to find the definition of sales that allows you to fall in love with it!

Your goal is to walk someone down a path to see if you can help them.

That's it!

Take It To H.E.A.R.T.

♥━━━━━♥

HEAR
Listen with genuine interest and sincerity.

EARN
Commit to walking the talk, showing up for them, and building loyalty.

ADVISE
Your expertise is extraordinary, and people need what you have.

RESPECT
Always consider their unique perspectives.

TRUST
Earn this, and they will come back again and again!

♥

Dora Rankin

Section Four
You Are The Expert

Dora Rankin

CHAPTER 11
Loving Your Business

Step one of falling in love with your business starts with *building your confidence.* Because most of us were raised to be "good girls" who never rocked the boat, we don't have the *practice* it takes to be a trailblazer. Because we are products of our environment, we live what we learn, and we learn what we live.

You Don't Have To Do Everything

If you are telling yourself that you have to do everything, consider this: You have a choice. Stop doing what you don't enjoy and use your time, energy, and focus to do the work you love. It's time to consider your options, some of which include hiring more staff and delegating the tasks that don't suit you.

I often help my clients with this.

Claim Your Power

A friend once told me that after six months of creating a business, sending out invoices, and successfully finishing numerous client projects, she was still telling people that she "was trying to start a business."

But when she held her first paid invoice in her hand, her mother looked at her and said, "You're no longer *trying,* dear. You're there! Give yourself some credit!"

If you only take one thing away from this book, let it be this: I've seen many women turn their businesses around by acknowledging their negative mindset and claiming their power. If this sounds familiar, it's time to make a concerted effort to change the channel!

Tangible Evidence

Sometimes, overcoming a significant difficulty and coming out on the other side proves—as tangible evidence—that we have what it takes to survive (or master) a new challenge. Witnessing our own resilience, courage, and ability to reinvent ourselves lays the groundwork for taking on new challenges, like starting or growing your business in new ways. By embracing these situations, overcoming them, and learning something in the process, we rebuild our confidence as we elevate our business.

Loving Your Business

Are you allowing your business to nurture you?

Or do you find yourself frustrated and feeling all of the complexity it adds to your life?

70% of women never make it past $100k /year

Do you know why? Mindset. Every time they say they won't make more money, they are reinforcing their lack of belief in themselves.

Identify any negative thoughts about yourself, your clients, or your business.

For me, it was that I'll never make enough money or that I'll never pass the $50K mark.

In the box below: Make note of anything that you need to stop saying or thinking about yourself, your clients, or your business.

You may wonder, when will I finally feel like an expert at what I do?

Like my friend's story, many of us need to push ourselves (or be pushed) into having an aha! moment to consider ourselves an "expert" at something. (I laughed the first time someone accused me of it!)

We realize our relevance by looking at the problems we solve for people while also noting the steps to get there. You will also begin to see it as you accumulate satisfied customers (and their testimonials!). Add these revelations to your journal entries and watch them multiply.

That's when your confidence will start growing exponentially and you'll realize, *I've got this!* Never underestimate your power combined with your ability to lead from the heart.

Remember this: Your mindset enables your strategy. Make a conscious shift to become an expert in your chosen field if you want to be taken seriously. Yes, helping clients with your unique solutions and collecting paid invoices will help get you there, but your certainty in knowing exactly what you do and don't offer will put your client's mind at ease.

Say this out loud and fill in the blank: "I'm an expert in/at _____ ."

Now, repeat it.

Say it again.

If you are stuck, try thinking through the results of working with you, how your customized solutions are different, and what your unfair advantage is.

Overcoming Challenges

At the end of this chapter, on page 107, take a moment to consider the challenges you've had to overcome in your lifetime. How have these situations prepared you for the future?

In the "You Are The Expert" matrix on page 108, answer all the questions, starting with which problems you solve.

Next Steps

Take a moment to think about what you do—or want to do—regarding how you spend (or will spend) your time building your business. If you are already working on your business, reflect on the past year.

What brought you the most joy in the last 365 days? Open your journal and take notes.

Start with the most recent quarter because that will be the easiest to remember. Then, go back a year, marking your quarters with dates. For each quarter, map out the most exciting experiences you've had. Why did you love it?

- Quarter 1:

- Quarter 2:

- Quarter 3:

- Quarter 4:

Do you see a common theme? What are you discovering about yourself, and what excites you about your business?

Better yet, why do you love your business? If you don't find anything exciting, that's vital information to have. Either you're in the wrong business or it's time to make some tweaks, like delegating work or realigning your offerings.

My Year In Review

As an example, here's my 2023 quarter-by-quarter recap. Look for the common thread!

- Q1: I was at a business retreat in Puerto

Rico and jumped at the chance to join Rachel Rodgers' Hello Seven coaching certification. This was exciting because I loved the diversity and purpose of the people around me.

- Q2: On a whim, I attended a business retreat with nine women business owners in France, and we saw Beyoncé in Paris! What was special about this experience was the women who joined me.

- Q3: I decided to publish a book called *The Heart Sell*, and thanks to the people in my circle, you're holding it in your hands right now! My dream team is helping me bring my dreams to life.

- Q4: I traveled the U.S., taking my clients on business retreats because these women light me up.

My common thread is the joy I find, who I surround myself with, and the relationships I've built.

Notice that I didn't mention my $100K months? That's because those are the byproduct of my love for the business, my ownership of purpose, and building heart-centered relationships.

Relationships

Let's return to your journal and create a page marked "Relationships."

Write down the names of the people who have positively influenced your life. I want you to think of the most important relationship you've had in your lifetime. Maybe it was with a parent. Or perhaps you had a loving relationship with a sibling, spouse, lover, or friend.

Because you knew it was a special relationship with a particular person, you probably nurtured it, making it a priority in your life. Now, I want you to consider your relationship with your business.

Do you love it unconditionally? Are you placing blame and putting expectations on it?

Just like our personal relationships, you can only get out of it what you put into it. This means that if you view client X (who is currently part of your business) or employee Z as a real pain in the butt, that is your reality.

Why?

Because your perception is your reality.

Who Are The Most Important People To You?

As you are thinking about the people who are important to you, take notes in your journal:

- What are their characteristics?
- Why are these relationships special, and why do you value them so much?

After reflecting on this list, ask yourself:

- What would happen if I looked at my business the same way I look at my most treasured relationships?
- How would that create a shift?
- Can falling in love with my business help me close the sale more often?

Write it down.

Hint: When you value and view your business through the same lens as your most treasured relationships, you will build your future in a whole new way.

That's The Heart Sell.

A Reframe For You

When someone asks what you do, how do you answer them? Please take note of your thoughts and write them down.

How would you answer if someone asked you to tell them what you do and why you do it?

Again, take note of your thoughts.

Notice the energy exchange. Is there a shift when answering the second question? That feeling is a great start to a new way of looking at your business—and your clients—and also makes a great ice-breaker question to ask a new connection at networking functions or coffee conversations.

I know you can do this!

Overcoming Challenges

What have you overcome in the past?

How have those challenges better prepared you for the future?

What do you need to overcome now?

You Are The Expert

What are the results of working with you?

How do you deliver these results differently?

What is your unfair advantage?

CHAPTER 12
How To Have A Non-Salesy Sales Conversation

So, you've realized you need to create opportunities to meet with potential clients by phone or in person, and you're worried about what to say because you don't want to come off as pushy.

That's why I talk about having non-salesy sales conversations, which are the backbone of The Heart Sell.

The goal of a sales conversation is to walk the other person down a path to see if you can help them. The intention is to build a relationship. You don't pitch unless you know with 100% certainty that you can help solve a pressing problem.

Let's go through The Heart Sell Method step by step. It will take you from step one of building rapport through to making your pitch.

The Heart Sell Method

When having a conversation with a potential client/customer, the seven steps are:

1. Build Rapport
2. Set The Agenda
3. Establish Outcomes
4. Create A Profile
5. Tell Your Story
6. Summarize
7. Give Your Pitch

1. Build Rapport. This is the easy part! In your initial conversation, do more listening than talking. Do some research before the call/meeting to make an authentic connection based on a common interest. (This makes everything easier!) You can do this by checking out their website and finding their social media profiles. It's always a good idea to start with LinkedIn. I often pull up someone's LI profile when chatting with them on the phone.

2. Set The Agenda. Share your intentions for the call. This could sound like: "I'm glad we found 30 minutes to connect today. My goal is to get to know you, including how you help people and what your projects and priorities are for the year."

3. Establish Outcomes. At the start of the conversation, transition with something like:

"Okay, great. It sounds like we have the same goals for the conversation. Typically, what I find during these sessions is one of three things happen:

- As we get to know each other, we find value in the relationship because one or both of us needs the other's services.
- We didn't really find anything this time, but we got to know each other, and now I can refer your services to other people.
- We've just skimmed the surface with these thirty minutes and realize we need to have another conversation.

Does that sound good to you?"

Be authentic. Adapt this script to fit your personality.

4. Create A Profile. There are three levels of questions when discussing a customer's business profile. Keep in mind that sometimes you won't make it to Level 3, and that's OK! In that case, you won't pitch. You will only pitch if you know 100% that you can solve a pressing problem of theirs.

LEVEL 1. This is a relaxed, getting-to-know-you conversation. Ask open-ended questions where you do more listening than talking. It's best if they go first. Your goal is to have them talk 80% of the time.

They will typically talk about what is currently happening to them. That's an excellent opportunity because your job is to uncover a problem you can solve with your product or service offering.

Examples include:
- "I would love to know about your business."
- "What got you to where you are today?"

LEVEL 2. Using your own personality and voice, ask questions unique to what *you* do based on their response in Level 1 with another set of questions. You're doing offline research!

Examples include:
- "What were you doing before you started this business?"
- "What challenges are you facing?"
- "Why is this business so important to you?"
- "What is keeping you up at night?"

LEVEL 3. We want to know how important or urgent the problem you've uncovered is. Keep listening to gather more information and help them recognize the pain and urgency.

Don't tell them your solution yet. If, and only if, you have a solution, continue with these questions. Come up with as many questions as you can. I have a list of about 30 to choose from, but obviously, I don't use them all. Over time, record the questions that work best for you and eliminate those that don't.

Examples include:
- "How have you tried to solve this problem?"
- "On a scale of 1 to 10, how big of a problem is this for you?"
- "When will you be committed and ready to make an investment to solve this?"

Three levels of profiling are significant because they will help you identify your potential client's "point of pain" or the problem they're having. When you uncover the pain, you'll know which solution to pitch.

5. Tell Your Story
- Keep it to 5-7 minutes
- Share your credentials to show you walk the talk
- Be vulnerable to build trust
- Make it personal enough that they get to know you

6. Summarize
Only summarize if you have reached the third level of profiling questions. It may sound like this: "I appreciated this call/meeting today. Based on everything you've shared, this is what I heard...
- X is important to you.
- You would love to have more/do less X.
- This is important because X is not working.

I think I can help you with that. Can I share my thoughts with you?"

7. Give Your Pitch
- Deliverables
- Timeline
- Price

The transition may sound like:
- "This is how you can work with me."
- "I work with clients in one of X ways."

An example statement: "You can work with me one-on-one or in a group. The timeline is either six months or a year, and the price point is between $10K and $25K."

Once you give them the deliverables, timeline, and price, *keep quiet.* Let them respond and ask questions because it means they are engaged.

If they have an objection, it's your opportunity to confirm their need to solve a problem. If you miss the mark, it's an opportunity to continue creating their profile.

Dora Rankin

CHAPTER 13
The Art Of Pitch-Free Prospecting (With Heart)

I find that women fall into one of two camps when it comes to prospecting. Some don't understand what it is and, therefore, have no idea how critical it is for business growth. Others have developed an aversion to prospecting based on previous experience with lackluster results.

The good news? When you lead from the heart, these issues are easy to resolve.

Prospecting

Prospecting has quite the reputation. Most of us have experienced bait-and-switch sales calls, annoying attempts to win us over in our DMs, or irrelevant sales proposals dumped in our email.

The majority of prospecting falls flat for two reasons. The first is a lack of authenticity. It's obvious that the person trying to connect with us isn't genuinely interested in getting to know us or understanding our needs. The second is what I call the in-your-face "Hail Mary" pitch, which tends to feel like a desperate plea for attention. This salesperson won't take no for an answer.

This is why I insist on pitch-free prospecting for my private clients and course students. When we move from audience identification to list building, we are looking for people we believe would be the right fit. The foundation of our prospecting work is finding people with whom we feel a genuine connection, admiration, or excitement.

The reality is, you don't want to work with everyone. Once you are clear about your target audience, you should surround yourself with people you love sharing space with day in and day out. And they should feel like it's a privilege to be invited to work with you. There is a time to extend that invitation, and prospecting is not that time.

Whether you are conducting strategic outreach, mingling at a mastermind, or attending an industry event, the goal of prospecting is simple. Your mission is to book a meeting (to have The Heart Sell conversation) and lead them down a path to uncover whether or not you can help them. (With enough practice, you will be able to lead this conversation on the spot!)

If you are not 100% certain you can help, then *you do not pitch*. This makes it all the more exciting when you uncover, through authenticity and mutual interest, that you *can* help. Then, you get to pitch with clarity and conviction and follow up with a timeline, deliverables, and price.

With my private clients and The Heart Sell course, I've developed a master prospecting script that provides a simple framework readily available and adaptable for strategic outreach and follow-ups. Once you have it, you or your team can modify it as needed without worrying about sounding salesy or sleazy. It is only six steps, and yes, I'm glad to share those steps with you.

Making Your Master Script: Six Steps For Success

Step 1: Know them before you know them

Research their most recent social media activity or find an article about them. Check out their website, then Google their name and business. LinkedIn is a great platform for this type of investigation. Look for something you genuinely have in common, and take note!

You will need a minimum of the following to commence outreach:

- Their name
- The name of their business/organization
- An article/post/achievement of interest—keep the link handy!
- An authentic commonality

This research should only take 20 minutes to complete. You can easily go down a rabbit hole, so be careful. Sometimes, you'll have the opportunity to reach out to someone you've met in person. If so, use that connection point as your commonality. Don't get stuck researching for hours, days, or weeks!

Next, it's time to write out your prospecting message. Leverage your research to complete steps two through six below.

Step 2: The introduction
Introduce yourself by name and greet them by name as well. No generic greetings! Think: "Hi, Natalie," versus "Hey, there." Explain who you are and why you chose them. (Be honest.) "I'd like to introduce myself, and I'm excited to connect because…"

Step 3: Identify a connection
Keep this simple! Example: "It looks like we run in some of the same circles."

Step 4: Give an authentic compliment
Keep it genuine, short, and specific. Example: "I love the birthday greetings in your card line."

Step 5: Make the ask
Don't sell or pitch! You are simply asking for a meeting/conversation. Example: "I would love to connect and discuss your projects and priorities for the coming months."

Step 6: Give them specific options
Make it easy for them to say yes by providing a few meeting dates and times. Example: "Does Monday at 10:00 a.m. EST or Wednesday at 11:00 a.m. work best for you? If you'd like to explore an alternative time, I am including my calendar link."

That's it!

Those are the steps.

Now, following the six steps, draft a personalized outreach message and send it to 10-20 people you'd like to work or partner with in the future. Keep going until you get calls booked. Ideally, you want to aim for 8-10 calls per week, but the most important thing is to get started! Perfection has no place in prospecting.

Prospecting messages are an area where you don't have to overthink or reinvent the wheel. Follow the six steps and hit send!

One message sent to the right inbox can land you a six-figure contract. Or a wholesale contract for 700 Nordstrom stores. If you want help getting started, The Heart Sell course could be a great fit, and there's a special offer for you inside the free book bundle (which can be found at dorarankin.com/book-bundle).

The book bundle also includes my *Non-Salesy Sales Conversation Guide*. Once you start booking calls, be sure to grab it, because it has a printable checklist for your calls.

Prospecting Research

Name of Individual

Business/Organization's Name

Source/link to article, post, or achievement

Notes (what piqued your interest)

What commonality can you leverage?

Dora Rankin

Section Five
Client Results

Dora Rankin

CHAPTER 14
Switching Gears

Even though women in the U.S. are far outpacing men in obtaining degrees and starting businesses, there's a statistic that concerns me.

Did you know that only 2% of women make more than $1,000,000 a year?[1] It's true—and we need to fix this.

Incredible Women

Now that we've taken the Delicious Dishes example as far as possible, I'd like to include some real-life examples of how The Heart Sell has helped my clients Amodhi and Lauren. The interviews in these coming chapters document the details of their businesses, passions, and results.

---

1. "Only 2% Of Women-Owned Businesses Break The $1 Million Mark—Here's How To Be One Of Them." https://www.forbes.com/sites/eilenezimmerman/2015/04/01/only-2-of-women-owned-businesses-break-the-1-million-mark-heres-how-to-be-one-of-them/

Let's start with Amodhi Weeresinghe. After working with her for a year, she contacted me one day to share her company's progress, saying, "Dora, I've increased my earnings tenfold, and it's because of the work we did together!"

I loved hearing that!

As I experienced that familiar flutter of joy from her feedback, it helped me make sense of the challenges I've been through because I know it's led me to become an instrument for women who are struggling with their businesses. Perhaps that's why the work I'm doing often feels divinely inspired.

Amodhi: The Risk-Taker And Innovator

As we sat down for a cup of coffee, Amodhi said, "Dora, as you recall, when we met a year ago, I was still working full-time, which involved 8-12 weeks of international travel. It was exhausting. I knew I wanted to start my own business, so I started doing some marketing and advertising work, offering social media, branding, and website design. I even entertained inquiries about developing custom software from my tech contacts.

"Even though these services were under the same umbrella, I soon felt scattered, and, as a solopreneur, there was a whirlwind of activity trying to keep up with it all. I was only earning $300 a month—not exactly the kind of money that warrants taking the leap.

"Three months later, demand had increased so much that I was earning $5,000 a month. I wondered if I should scale my business or stay at my current job. Looking back, I don't know how I did it all."

I sipped my coffee and said, "Yes, I remember how difficult those growing pains were for you."

She replied, "It quickly became evident that I needed to go full-time with my business and maybe even hire people!"

Question #1: *What* Do You Want, And *Why* Do You Want It?

"Dora," Amodhi admitted, "our first conversation was intense. My business was growing quickly, and I couldn't decide what to do next! I needed a clear roadmap. I didn't understand anything about passion and purpose. You had to teach me that.

"I was responding in a reactionary way to client requests instead of standing back and proactively creating a company that could define my life for the next 30 years. I needed to put some thought into that!"

"Ah, yes," I replied, "the importance of asking '*What* do you want, and *why* do you want it?' Both are directly related to your passion and purpose."

Amodhi laughed. "Exactly. When you asked me *why* I wanted to have a marketing business, I listed *getting away from corporate* as my main reason. But, as you told me, that's not a good reason to dedicate your heart and soul to creating something.

"So, I thought about it for a moment, and before I could answer, you said, 'And don't tell me it's about *earning a living* either. There's more to it than that!'

"I remember thinking, *Oh, no. I'm in trouble because I don't know the answer!*"

We laughed.

"Well," I reminded her, "I designed that exercise to make you think about your passion and purpose. That's your 'Why,' and no one else can answer it for you. Sometimes it takes some thought, but you were willing to do the work."

"Yes," Amodhi said, smiling. "It took me a moment to get there, but I drove home thinking about that question. And I also thought about what you said concerning the 'mega-deal prices' we were offering and how that could be a recipe for disaster."

We clinked our coffee cups with a knowing nod.

"I was at an important precipice where I had an *opportunity* to stand back, take a breath, and ask myself, 'Amodhi, *what* do you want, and *why* do you want it?' I owed it to myself to do some self-reflection and think long and hard about the future I was about to carve out for myself.

"Thankfully, you sent me those documents about yearly goals and trajectories. As I started filling them out, I got overwhelmed with my own offerings! That was a huge clue that something was off.

"My business model felt unsustainable for three reasons. The first was that I didn't have the bandwidth for all those offerings, which meant I'd have to scale up quickly and consider hiring people.

"The second was that, as I mentioned, I was

accepting anything thrown my way. That had an air of desperation surrounding it, and I didn't want to start a business with that kind of energy."

I smiled and asked, "And the third thing?"

"My mindset wasn't where it needed to be. That, combined with overwhelmingly fast growth, jammed my thinking. It made me question whether I was capable—or ready—and comfortable presenting myself as an expert because I knew that was the next step.

"The thought of continuing to work the way I'd been working felt exhausting and painful."

"Believe it or not," I said, "that's a good sign. It means you weren't on the right path."

Question #2: What Are Your Assets?

"Everything started feeling so complicated," Amodhi reminisced, "I wanted something that felt more *natural*—even joyful. When I began focusing on the industry I knew the most about, I contemplated switching my area of specialization to fintech (finance and technology). But I was still considering creating the marketing agency—in addition to working in fintech.

"I got so frustrated that I let the idea go, shifting my thoughts to getting tasks done around the house. As I started to make myself lunch, I stopped dead in my tracks.

"That's when it happened. Like a lightbulb. Boom!"

"What?" I asked.

"Once I calmed my mind, I started thinking about offering customized software development *instead of* the marketing agency. That was my aha! moment!"

"Don't you just love those?" I said with a smile. "Eureka!"

"When I spoke to you about it days later," Amodhi added, "we discussed how this shift would offer more stability for my company because everyone knows corporate *marketing* budgets are the first thing on the chopping block during economic downturns. But in my experience, no one touches the tech budgets, which are usually flush with cash.

"When those factors came together for me, my 'why'—which had been simmering just under the surface—immediately appeared! I knew I wanted to help other, often marginalized women business owners in need of scaling their businesses, and I wanted to do it with customized software solutions."

I raised my glass. "Aha!"

CHAPTER 15
Don't Take Failure Personally

After we took a moment to high-five, Amodhi said, "The next step for me became clear: I needed to realize my value and charge rates that were commensurate with my expertise. I also knew I needed to hire a larger team to support me, so I had to create a pricing structure that covered their salaries.

"In a meeting with several great developers I'd known over the years, I put together a financial plan. Then my $5,000 monthly retainers became $25,000."

"You've always been a risk-taker," I said with a grin.

Question #3:
What Were Your Growing Pains?

"Dora, things were starting to gel quickly until I hit an unexpected challenge, which got my attention! This represented my need for a major mindset shift as the new CEO. I realized I was single-handedly bottlenecking the business because I was like an octopus with my tentacles in everything, micromanaging every project instead of letting my team take the lead."

Smiling, I asked, "And what did you do next?"

"You told me to fire myself from every department!"

I replied, "Well, it worked, didn't it?"

Laughing, she continued, "As a visual person, the organizational chart we created laid everything out that I needed to see. We listed every job, employee, vendor, and service provider. Then, I could see where the bottlenecks were happening and who was the cause—*me!*"

"But you liked what came next, didn't you?" I asked. "After all, you got to pick the job you wanted most."

"And that's when everything came together for me! I knew my job as CEO would be focused on business development because no one can sell a business' services and solutions better than the owner.

"Because of the systems we've implemented, I'm working less and making more money.

"Not only that," Amodhi added, "but I've made everyone in my team a leader in their own right. Instead of having an organizational chart with one person at the top, ours looks more like a network where everyone takes responsibility for their department and job.

"It works great for us."

Question #4: How Did The Heart Sell Make The Difference?

"Dora, I've got to hand it to you. Once I knew my 'what' and 'why,' everything fell into place. I knew which products to offer, who to hire, and how to help my community, especially women and non-binary people of color.

"It's rare to find this segment of people working in tech as engineers, etc., but it's almost *unheard of* to find a woman who owns her own company in this field. You helped me do that."

When I asked Amodhi about the most significant impact for her, she answered, "I love that the pressure's off because now that I know the 80/20 Rule works, everything has become easier.

"Even my employees agree. Because we have a solid plan, we know how to react whenever we get stuck on a task or a customer service hiccup. We have fun documenting our weekly goals and taking turns ringing the bell on Fridays when we meet them.

"One thing we talk about is your Q x Q = R formula, which is our go-to business development strategy. We have a chart showing that the *quality* of our leads, multiplied by targeted *quantities,* will give us the *results* we're looking for. It makes meeting our goals so much easier."

"How are you using it?" I asked.

"If we don't close a sale, we know the quality of the lead was off and we course-correct, usually by maintaining or increasing the quantity side of the formula with our pipeline of leads. That's what helps us find our perfect customer.

"It works because we no longer take 'failures' personally. When a potential client doesn't sign with us, we ask them why. At first, it took guts to implement this, but it's important to have data to back up all our hard work. We're constantly measuring successes and non-successes.

"Sometimes their reason is tied to the *Know, Like, and Trust Principle* because they went with another company they know better. We know we can't compete with that, and to be honest, that's the reason we've won several bids, so we realize it wasn't our turn this time.

"But in every case," she continued, "we are backed by the 80/20 Rule to decide how to increase business through an outreach effort that results in relationship building. That's the one we lean on the most. I recently joined a professional women's group, resulting in several leads and potential partners.

"In addition, my employees personally choose the networking opportunities they prefer to join and attend."

Question #5: What Were The Results?

"As a result of raising our prices to become competitive in the market, I've been able to take on fewer clients while providing higher-quality problem-solving. I love doing intricate work that involves creating innovative solutions because I don't believe in the word 'no.'"

"I'm sure your clients appreciate that!"

"I believe they do. And I've also learned that it's the business owner's knowledge and excitement that closes the sale because that passion becomes the steam engine that makes you excited to start your day. Dora, one reason I've enjoyed working with you is that you were able to tap into that and advise me on the best ways to exude that confidence in my client sales calls."

"People love to see that!" I replied. "It's contagious!"

"Plus," Amodhi added, "our results include being able to hire more female engineers. We recently hired someone from Microsoft. She decided to make the move despite having to take a pay cut because she believes in our mission, which centers around empowering underrepresented people. We want to change the business landscape."

"That's awesome," I said, beaming.

"And finally, the most measurable result is based on what I mentioned earlier. My earnings have increased *tenfold*, and it's been life-changing money for me. Because of it, I can surround myself with a custom-built team and make a difference in my community and industry."

"Congratulations, Amodhi."

Amodhi Weeresinghe

Founder, HCL Designs

— 99 —

Working with Dora was transformative.

Dora's guidance was instrumental in refining our offerings, reorganizing our team structure, and making some challenging but necessary decisions.

This led to a significant increase in our deal size—from an average of $35K to a range of $70K-250K.

She also coached me on setting boundaries within the team, allowing me to focus more on VIP clients and business development, and trained my COO in business development strategies.

— 99 —

Dora Rankin

CHAPTER 16
Charging What You're Worth

At this point in my story, I'd like to introduce another client who has enjoyed excellent results using The Heart Sell concepts. Her name is Lauren Schmidt, and she is a global education consultant who was in business for years before we met.

Lauren: The International Sensation

During our second-year post-game analysis, I said, "Lauren, can you believe how many students you're helping? And who knows how that will trickle down through their families? You're helping them rewrite their legacies for generations to come."

Lauren helps students who want to earn their degrees by garnering scholarships and financial aid from countries like China, Tanzania, Brazil, Kenya, the U.K., Rwanda, Greece, Turkey, and the U.S. She does this by helping her students identify and develop a unique "passion project" for use in their college essays.

Question #1: *What* Do You Want, And *Why* Do You Want It?

When Lauren came to me two years ago, she said, "Dora, can you help me figure out how I can get organizations to pay me to help students from abroad? These students are serious about their educations, targeting universities like MIT, Stanford, Harvard, Yale, Cornell, Brown, and others."

"Wow," I replied. "You're dealing with some heavy hitters. Let's do this! I love helping people go after what they want!"

"The good news is I'm clear about what I want and passionate about my sense of purpose," Lauren stated, "but I need to figure out how to make all the right connections. To give you an example of the kind of work I do, last month, I had a student named Zahara from India who is passionate about the criminal justice system, and she also loves music.

"I helped Zahara develop a project showcasing a playlist she curated on Spotify in Hindi, Swahili, and English. She uses it as musical therapy to facilitate conversations about mental health in her community."

"That's incredible, Lauren," I said.

Question #2: What Are Your Assets?

"The global impact projects that my students develop have successfully helped them obtain scholarships with their college admissions applications. But I want to be able to support myself and my children as a newly divorced mother."

"Zahara's project was important to me because I'm concerned by the mental health statistics in young people today," Lauren added. "I believe part of the epidemic of anxiety and depression levels among this demographic is due to a lack of clarity regarding their passion and purpose.

"The goal is to help them find fulfilling work they're excited about. Because of the scholarship I helped her obtain, Zahara was accepted by Harvard. She enrolled last week!"

"Wow," I answered, taking a beat to let that sink in. "You're doing important work, giving young adults opportunities they wouldn't get otherwise."

Question #3:
How Did The Heart Sell Make A Difference?

"When we created a plan to have you meet with private college admissions agencies and college administrators across the country," I reflected, "you thought it was too ambitious, remember? But I knew you'd grow and nurture those relationships, helping hundreds, maybe thousands of students live their dreams by living yours."

"Yes," Lauren agreed, "your strategic plan sounded a little intimidating at first, but once I got started, I knew we were on the right path."

As Lauren smiled, I said, "I want to tell you something, and I really need you to hear me."

"Okay," Lauren answered.

"Get comfortable for a moment in your chair and lean back. Then close your eyes, take a deep breath, and concentrate on the sound of my voice."

She shrugged her shoulders, closed her eyes, and relaxed.

"Are you paying attention?" I asked.

She nodded.

"Lauren," I assured her, "you are more powerful than you know."

Her eyes opened brightly. A grin replaced her look of focus.

She got the message. And it planted a seed.

Question #4: What Were Your Growing Pains?

Days into our working relationship, I realized a large part of our challenge hinged on building Lauren's self-confidence. This is common with the women I work with who are just starting out or struggling with their businesses.

When I mentioned this, she confessed, "In the not-so-distant past, when I worked for someone else, I was so low that I'd ask permission to do the most minor things. I was afraid to take the initiative to spend money—even if it was budgeted for my department!

"That's why I've put up with a low-paying job. I don't like talking about money because my folks taught me that it was improper to do so. Especially for a 'lady.'"

I nodded. "I know how uncomfortable you are talking about money. But if you're a business person, making money is the point, isn't it?"

She smiled.

"Lauren, I'm glad you trust me enough to hear me and address some of the things that have been holding you back. That's when the most impactful changes can happen."

Question #5: What Were The Results?

Let's fast forward six months to illustrate how I helped Lauren grow her business.

One morning, as we met for coffee, Lauren smiled and said, "So, here we are, Dora. When we met, I was at ground zero with my self-esteem, my financial issues, and a complicated divorce. I was scared!

"But a month after signing with you, we had a solid plan that included connecting with college administrators on LinkedIn by using Navigator. I sent about 20 messages a day until I snagged five quality calls with top-ranking universities.

"One of the organizations I was prospecting commented that this was a service they needed and discovering me was like finding a diamond in the rough. My next client, a gentleman from Yale, told me I made his job easier. *Can you imagine my gratitude?*"

I smiled.

CHAPTER 17
You've Come A Long Way

Lauren sat down and opened her laptop, showing me how her Sales & Lead Tracker helped her accomplish her next milestone. (The tracker is available at dorarankin.com when you purchase The Heart Sell Course.)

She said, "Things began to change quickly with the *number* of qualified connections I made. In a mere four weeks of adopting your formulas and principles, I had a signed contract with a new school—that started as a cold call—and I was scheduled for a Tedx talk.

"It all started with the Lead Tracker, which is super easy to use. Turning a cold lead into a warm one, then a hot one, made me realize the progress I was making. And it's all tied to the systems you've taught me!"

She laughed and said, "I must admit that sometimes I have a Dora tape playing in my head."

"Oh no!" I said laughing, flailing my hands.

"No, really! I especially like the time you told me that the goal of everything we do is to reinforce our belief in ourselves while celebrating our successes. So, whenever I'm in a challenging situation, I try to look for the positive things that have happened, and they begin to stack up in my brain!"

I replied, "It's hard to stay frustrated when you realize all the positive things happening in your favor."

"When we started," Lauren continued, "I was getting paid $20 an hour to help 30 students. This meant I made about $1,000 a week—and I was happy to get it—even though I barely got by as a single mother of three.

"But once we started working together, you taught me how to raise my rates, gradually, and now I'm making $4,000 a week helping *two* students with their college admissions essays.

"Because of that shift, I have more time to spend with my children, and we have a more comfortable lifestyle because their mother isn't always stressed about paying the bills."

"Incredible," I answered, shaking my head. "You've come a long way, Lauren."

"What seems even more miraculous," she added, "is that over the past two years, I've secured $8 million in financial aid for my students. One student in particular received $2 million in aid, and she's studying at Duke. It's hard to believe, but she had so many offers, she had a tough time choosing which university to attend!"

"I know you love seeing these young adults foster a sense of pride around their projects," I said, "which translates into watching them grow more confident in themselves. These projects give them a leg up."

"They do," Lauren agreed, "and The Heart Sell method showed me that it's not about in-your-face sales or ego-driven presentations. *It's about showing up and having conversations.* I love helping other people understand the solutions I'm passionate about.

"Now, when I meet with a potential client, I start by asking a lot of questions, then I develop a customized approach to their problems. I know my services so well, I can often do this on the spot!"

"That's great," I replied. "It gets easier over time."

"You've taught me a lot—and you're right, there's no shame in hearing the word 'no.'

"You can't go wrong if you speak from the heart, take time to understand people's objections, and address how you can solve their issues. If they're still not convinced my services are right, I chalk it up as a learning experience to be better prepared next time.

"I used to measure each sales conversation using the 'winning' or 'losing' model, but that isn't a strategy for success if the goal is reinforcing your belief in yourself and your services.

"Dora," she added, "thank you for believing in me at a time when I didn't. It's clear that you genuinely enjoy helping women business owners thrive."

"Well, I showed you the way, Lauren, but you did all the hard work. You jumped in and started building relationships that will last *years*. Now, each school year is a matter of lather, rinse, and repeat because you have pinpointed and nurtured those connections."

More Good News

"Oh! I just remembered I have news to share! Yesterday, I was invited to New York City to speak with a panel of professionals, including a Nobel Peace Prize winner."

"Congratulations!" I said, gasping with excitement. "See what happens when you find the key to your heart?"

"If you would have told me two years ago that this would be my life now," Lauren admitted, "I would have told you you're crazy."

She became serious for a moment. "Dora," Lauren said, looking me right in the eye, "when I talk to family and friends about my connection with you, I always find myself saying it's heart-centered because, from the beginning, you've *heard and seen me.*"

"It's been a pleasure, Lauren."

She added, "After all you've been through, you are brave enough to see and believe in yourself, which gives me a solid role model in knowing that I can transform myself the same way."

"Lauren," I reminded her, "it's all about the value *you* bring to the world. You're finally being paid what you're worth. Remember, your solutions are making your clients' lives easier: the parents, the students, *and* the college administrators."

I pointed to her and said, "You're helping a lot of people because *you're more powerful than you know!*"

Lauren Schmidt

Founder, A Tree That Grows

———— 99 ————

I went from having no business to doing a TedTalk and being on a panel with someone who won a Nobel Peace Prize.

Just this week, I am closing 3 contracts.

What Dora taught me is, if I want the magic, it is about doing the work ... and having a sense of calmness to this process.

It doesn't feel like I am leaving anything up to chance. This is something I can do repeatedly and continue to build.

It feels like I have taken control of my business.

———— 👌 ————

Dora Rankin

Section Six
The Sky's The Limit

Dora Rankin

CHAPTER 18

How To Build A Relationship-Driven, Revenue-Rich Business

Earlier, I mentioned that after working 20 years in corporate America, earning a meager poverty-level salary while accepting bonuses and promotions that made me feel like I was being trafficked, I needed to create a business. So, after my birthday dinner with my sister, I began to plan for the new company I was forming.

I was facing two monumental fears. The first was, after being a vice president at the bank, I couldn't imagine building a business that brought in that kind of (replacement) money.

Perhaps more importantly, I didn't want to earn that type of money only to sign up for the kind of stressors that would trigger burnout, break my spirit, or damage my health—and relationships—in any way.

After all, don't big-money salaries tend to align with careers that run at breakneck speed?

Creating A Strategic Growth Plan

When I started my coaching business, my first project brought in $1,500—and I was happy to receive my first payment! But once I realized it took a month to earn, I quickly understood that $18K a year wouldn't cover my business and personal expenses.

I knew I needed to lean on the process I'd been trained on for decades by putting a plan in place and following through. It was time for me to own my expertise, trust my process, and admit I had everything I needed to make life-changing amounts of money—my way.

Here are a few of the secrets to my success (and my clients' success too).

Secret #1: Your audience is more important than your offer (what you're selling).

If you find yourself changing offers or pivoting frequently, your *solutions* are probably not the problem. More than likely, you need to focus on knowing your audience well enough so you can *identify* them, *find* them, and *build relationships* with them.

Secret #2: Your strategy is only as good as your mindset.

If limiting beliefs are holding you down, you

will struggle. A $27 solution is just as hard to sell as a $27,000 solution, and both are easier to sell once you consider yourself an expert! I spend a great deal of time on mindset with my private clients, and the ROI (return on investment) is always worth it!

Secret #3: Always have a 1:1 coach.

Even if you know the road map to a successful, sustainable business, you can't see your blind spots—*but your coach can.* Every time I think I can go without, I find myself struggling. Take it from me: always have a coach.

When I first started my business, I was comfortable with the idea of earning a living in a salary range I was familiar with. But in the back of my mind, I heard my sister's anthem: "You're the golden goose! If you can do it for others, why not yourself?"

Soon, I had $10K months and felt like my business was on fire. As I continued to teach about the infinite possibilities of growth, I started earning $100K months, and so did my clients!

In fact, one of my clients, who'd been in business for years before we met, earned over a million dollars—for the first time—last year, and she credits The Heart Sell for her success.

How did she do it? She deeply understood her audience. She made a decision to own her economic power, and she believed in herself. She invested in one-on-one support, and when she experienced uncertainty, she always had me beside her to unblock the barriers.

Making life-changing amounts of money doesn't have to be complicated. As with all my clients, we started simply by creating a list of potential leads and inviting them to non-salesy, "getting to know you" conversations. Several of those conversations led to a sale. Then she repeated that process again and again, and I watched her confidence levels soar. The sky's the limit!

Creating Goals

As you look at your products and services, I don't want you to think about what you can make if you sell them. Instead, I want you to work backward by thinking about how much money you want to make when you sell them. From there, you will be able to break down how many you need to sell to meet your goals.

Then, when you know how much you need to sell to meet your goal, I want you to break this down for the next four quarters. Start with specific goals for the next 90 days and go from there.

Real Simple Revenue Goals

(1)
My Offer

(2)
What I want to make from this offer ($)

(3)
Offer Price

(4)
How many do I need to sell?
(Divide answer 2 by answer 3)

Goals: Next 90 Days

♥

- ♥ _____
- ♥ _____
- ♥ _____

Goals: Next 4 Quarters

♥

- ♥ _____
- ♥ _____
- ♥ _____
- ♥ _____

Meet & Exceed Your Goals

High Level, High Results, Your Highest Potential

When setting your goals, consider this: I was never supposed to be the woman who learned how to have $100K sales months while teaching other women to do the same. I was the kid who always bent the rules to see what I could get away with—without getting caught.

If I can do this, you can too.

Benchmarks and Breakthroughs

When I welcome women into the Heart Sell course, I kick things off with a Benchmark and Breakthrough virtual retreat. During this time together, we clarify and simplify goals, signature frameworks, and flagship offers, laying the foundation for six-figure quarters, months, and contracts.

So many people come in with offers and frameworks that they have poured endless amounts of time, energy, and money into. My job is to get them to strip away all the shiny objects so they come to the course prepared to implement everything I teach them. We start with the mindset exercise to set the stage and quickly identify the goals they *really* want to reach.

I invite you to review a sample of The Heart Sell framework for you to refer to. It illustrates the key focus points and steps to success. You can download a copy for you to complete at dorarankin.com/book-bundle.

The Heart Sell framework helps me guide my clients because we've proven that they will achieve their goals if they do the following:

1. Deeply understand their audience. What that means, specifically, is that they can identify their ideal client clearly enough to actually find them and test if they are a good fit. If not, they go back to step one—audience identification—to fine-tune.

2. Describe their offer in three ways (and three ways only): timeline, deliverables, and price. That's all that's needed to start a conversation and uncover how you can help your potential client. Most business owners bog people down with too much information when sharing how they can help them. Simplicity sells.

3. Commit to outreach for their ideal clients, partners, and ecosystem players. To do this, they must build (and maintain) lists and prospecting scripts that allow them to connect to the right people, invite them into conversations, and build relationships.

Remember, *complexity kills sales.* It shouldn't require bells and whistles to close a sale, just authenticity and heart. Building relationships is part of human nature, yet it's a novel approach in business these days. Use this as your competitive advantage!

Reward Yourself

As you start your brand new business, land your first client, or enjoy your first $100K month, remember this: If you aren't grateful for each accomplishment, you're doing yourself a disservice. (Sometimes, we can be our own worst enemies.)

In other words, when you score a significant goal but fail to enjoy the win and appreciate how far you've come with each new project or financial gain, you're acting like a hamster on a treadmill. You're treating your business—and yourself—like it's never "good enough."

If you want to be treated that way, you could just stay in corporate America. Right? So, be careful how you talk to yourself when "comparing and despairing."

Make it a practice to find joy in everyday successes—small and large—because your positive energy will radiate to your clients, employees, and community.

Give yourself permission to reward yourself for your success! For one of my favorite clients, that meant purchasing a bike she'd wanted since she was a kid. (It was purple, with streamers!) Another client books a massage every time she has a micro or macro win.

Conversely, if you're stuck because something isn't working, continue to ask the "What Do You Want?" question until you find a solution that does. Weathering disappointments that require another level of improvement and appreciating the solutions we uncover helps us witness our ability to learn, grow, and lead.

Then, we continue to gain confidence for the next big project.

Playing The Long Game

As a business owner, *you* are your most valuable asset. No one else in the company knows the hours (and years!) you've put into it. As you continue to grow, one of my biggest suggestions is to always *invest in yourself.*

If you get nothing else from this book, please consider hiring a coach to help you with your business struggles. (It doesn't have to be me!) The adage is true: Sometimes, we're just too close to a problem to see it. That's where another perspective can be invaluable.

Learning By Example

In the case studies I've highlighted, you've witnessed the stories of two successful businesswomen who were stuck at a certain level of growth because they needed to see their day-to-day through a different lens. Believe it or not, that's often the first stumbling block with business owners, and fortunately, I was able to help these women.

As I've mentioned, a business coach's job is to ask their clients the right questions to help them identify myriad possibilities in finding a solution. Having a fresh perspective helps a business owner uncover problems they may not have known they had.

After all, you can't fix something if you don't acknowledge that it's broken.

If we are to grow as businesspeople *and* human beings, we all need a mindset shift from time to time, especially if we tend to be stubborn and set in our ways (like me).

In summary, consider hiring a reputable business coach if you are stuck or struggling—and ask them to help you *confidentially* if that's important to you.

CHAPTER 19
Women Who Soar

In today's world, with all the noise and hyperactive marketing tactics, relationship-driven sales can stand out as a novel USP (unique selling point). It starts with making the shift to realize that marketing is carried out behind the scenes while sales outreach needs to be your frontline strategy.

Yes, online marketing is accessible and exciting. It's easy to get online, follow the trends, and feel like you're building a business.

However, while social media trends can be fun, and you should use the ones you like, realizing *they aren't enough* is the first step in building sustained, consistent revenue. Trends are simply short-term sensations with expiration dates built in. The problem is, you don't know when the milk will sour.

Even the most qualified social media experts get stuck trying to keep up with the trends, but do you want to know a secret? The modern marketing landscape changes so rapidly that you can lose steam just trying to keep up.

So, What's The Good News?

Your ability to lead from the heart is more powerful than you know. Some of my most successful clients spend little to no time on social media marketing because they focus on *sales first*. As a solo or small team-supported female founder, coach, or consultant, your time and energy are your greatest assets, so you must manage them wisely.

Whether you're a solopreneur or a team-building superwoman, you need to free up space to master relationship-driven sales. Then, you can train others to follow your lead. After that, your sales will grow and your return on investment will multiply. It's a proven forever strategy.

Remember, large businesses dedicate entire teams and sizable budgets to managing their marketing machines. One person in the sales department—who follows the sales process—can generate enough revenue to sustain the entire company. *That* is the power of sales.

The Bottom Line

Everyone's looking for that magic bullet, that new trend or quick fix that will make them rich. It's all too easy to have "shiny object syndrome," wasting time and money looking for a magic pill to boost sales.

Do you remember the days of infomercials and QVC? They were trends that were replaced by TikTok and Instagram. Why? Because TV (early tech) didn't have the reach or staying power once the Internet took off.

That's why staying agile and growing your business with long-term, proven methods is a smart move that will pay dividends. Relationship-driven sales have been around for ages for a reason: they work.

By using these methods, you will soon be enjoying mega contracts as *your* new reality.

Getting Out Of Your Comfort Zone

By prioritizing business relationships (and people), you can make life-changing amounts of money while living your purpose—built on passion. I've watched clients who came to me with no business earn their first $60K contracts or enjoy their first million-dollar years.

In the pages of this book, you've learned how to find your passion and purpose, define your audience, build a weekly outbound growth strategy, have non-salesy sales conversations, and stabilize your marketing. You've also discovered how to build your confidence, see yourself as an expert, and appreciate the advantages of the 80/20 Rule, which explains why one-on-one meetings are so powerful!

You're well on your way and have everything you need to implement a scalable, sustainable business, and $100K months are completely within reach. Now it's up to you.

You can close this book and go back to the same old, same old, or decide today—in this moment—to start a new chapter in your life.

I will ask you this one more time: What are you passionate about, and what do you want to do with your one precious life?

You don't have to settle for making *just enough* money to survive. You deserve more. So take it! Financial freedom is found through The Heart Sell, so go steal the show!

The Heart Sell

Dora Rankin

About The Author

Dora Rankin is a business growth advisor, fractional CEO, and public speaker. Her superpowers include helping women entrepreneurs become financially free by growing their businesses and their revenue.

She credits her mother's teachings of "big love" for her decision to dedicate her life to helping women entrepreneurs. Once a single mother working through 12-step recovery, Dora became the caregiver for her ailing mother while working her way up the corporate ladder at a prestigious bank.

Shocked at the way women were treated in that culture, she allowed her mother's love to be her guiding light, choosing to help women discover their purpose while teaching them how to optimize profits and minimize risk.

With over 25 years of experience, Dora has developed a strong reputation for building high-performing leaders, CEOs, teams, and partnerships. Now, in the pages of this book, she shares her secrets with you.

In *The Heart Sell,* Dora shares how a "sales first" approach is imperative for savvy businesswomen who want to create consistent, sustainable revenue. As someone who has constantly disrupted trends—like current online marketing campaigns that promise more than they deliver—Dora leans on proven, relationship-driven sales methods that have withstood the test of time.

www.ingramcontent.com/pod-product-compliance
Lightning Source LLC
Chambersburg PA
CBHW020653220526
45464CB00001B/424